MURDER INC

MURDER INC

THE MAFIA'S HIT MEN IN NEW YORK CITY

GRAHAM K. BELL

THE
History
PRESS

Published by The History Press
Charleston, SC 29403
www.historypress.net

Manufactured in the United States

ISBN 978.1.60949.135.2

Bell, Graham.
Murder, Inc. : the Mafia's hit men in New York City / Graham Bell.
p. cm.
ISBN 978-1-60949-135-2
1. Mafia--New York (State)--New York--History--20th century. 2. Mafiosi--New York
(State)--New York--History--20th century. 3. Assassins--New York (State)--New York--
History--20th century. 4. Organized crime--New York (State)--New York--History--20th
century. I. Title.
HV6452.N72M34185 2010
364.152'309227471--dc22
2010042769

Contents

CONTENTS

INTRODUCTION

The body of one of the most efficient murderers in history, and certainly the best criminal informant in the life of the American republic, lay prone on one of the ledges of the Half Moon Hotel, on Coney Island, New York. It was November 12, 1941, and the corpse in question was that of Abraham "Kid Twist" Reles.

Before he died, Reles had created headlines throughout America concerning the existence of a strange, lethal organization called Murder, Incorporated (or Murder, Inc.). This was, literally, the hit squad of the vast criminal organization that later generations, sated with the film *The Godfather*, would call the Mafia. Before he died, Reles had admitted to more than twenty murders; thanks to his testimony, seven men took the long and fatal journey to the electric chair in Sing Sing prison. One of these men, Lepke Buchalter, is so far the only top-echelon boss of the Mafia ever to be executed. Another of this number, Harry Strauss—also known as "Pittsburgh Phil," "Big Harry" and "Pep"—is perhaps the most able hit man the Mafia ever produced, having taken out, by the most conservative estimates, more than one hundred men.

When Reles's body was discovered on the ledge of the Half Moon Hotel, a legend was created—of Murder, Inc. and of Reles, "the canary who could sing but could not fly."

Chapter 1

GENESIS IN SICILY, EXODUS TO AMERICA

The story of Murder, Inc., as well as the death of Reles, starts many thousands of miles away from the bustle of New York, and hundreds of years before the war year of 1941, on the Mediterranean island of Sicily.

Conquered by the Romans in the centuries before the coming of the Caesars under Augustus, the island was seen by its mainland masters as a gigantic breadbasket whose sole role was to provide bread for the teeming multitude of the metropolis of Rome. By the coming of Augustus, local rule on the island had been savagely crushed, rebellions had been led by slaves and city-states such as Syracuse had been brutally oppressed—the losers, if they were lucky, were sent as slaves to the various mines in Sicily or, if they were not, were sent to the Coliseum in Rome, where their deaths were watched with sadistic fascination by the Roman mob; sometimes they were made to taste the agonies of crucifixion, a punishment known for centuries before the body of Christ was hung in Jerusalem.

The Sicilians ever afterward hated and feared any government put over them as being one of exploiters from foreign lands, whose main intention was to wring as much wealth out of the island as possible. They were usually right. Over the next few centuries, the island went through a bewildering change of rulers: Greeks from Byzantium, Vandals from

North Africa, Ostrogoths, Arabs and Normans—all came to the land to exploit but rarely to build. Even the savage war criminal Richard I, the king of England, the Lionheart, landed on the island on his murderous way to the third crusade and, to the surprise of no one who knew him, created havoc.

Sicily was booted backward and forward by the great powers of Europe, one country never staying for too long as the imperial power. The result was that, unlike in the rest of Europe, there was no settled period of law and governance on this island. The results of these facts were obvious: the landlords, the natural leaders of the community, began to expand their powers in ways that the kings and parliaments of the rest of the continent (in the northwest, anyway) had managed to curtail. The beleaguered peasants of the island, progressively tyrannized, began to form local self-help organizations, which were later given the generic title of "the Mafia," a name whose meaning has been discussed for centuries. These groups attacked the landowners' estates and servants, warning them of the folly of their ways.

What happened next was the classic lesson to anyone wishing to understand the rudiments of divide and rule: the landowners quietly suggested to the local bands of Mafiosi that it would be more advisable to join together and mutually terrorize and plunder the peasants and townsmen.

With the enlightened self-interest that has always been one of the attributes of able men, the local gangs accepted these conditions with alacrity, and the Sicilians soon found themselves plundered not only by their landlords but also by their own erstwhile protectors.

The reunification of Italy in the mid-nineteenth century, so lusted after by the romantics in so many nations, had very little effect in Sicily, where the terrorization of the population continued apace.

The huge emigration from Sicily and Italy to the United States in the nineteenth and early twentieth centuries (the more ambitious members of the population, like millions from the rest of Europe) not only presented the New World with thousands of industrious workers—men and women who would enrich their new homeland with their cultures and industry—but also allowed the criminal gangs of Sicily to follow their compatriots to the New World and, as in the old one, exploit them mercilessly.

Little Italy during the height of Italian immigration. *Courtesy of the George Grantham Bain Collection, Library of Congress.*

It must be pointed out here and now that this book is a volume, for the most part, about treachery, murder and greed, and many of the main characters will be of Italian or Sicilian stock. It must be noted, however, notwithstanding films like *The Godfather* or *Goodfellas*, that the overwhelming number of these much maligned people were and are absolutely respectable, hardworking and honest. Their culture has enriched their country to an unimaginable degree. Their labor has cleared the forests; built the canals, railways and highways; and constructed the schools that have enabled the people of the Italian peninsula to pull themselves up by their bootstraps and produce American worthies such as Francis Ford Coppola, Robert De Niro, Rudolph Giuliani and Rocky Marciano to name but a few. (In case anybody thinks that these people were nothing but ignorant layabouts, it should be pointed out that along with the Irish Americans, the Italian Americans produced from their ranks most of the men and women who fought for their countries in both world wars and Korea and who followed the trumpet in a way few other ethnicities did in the war in Vietnam. The author would like to take this opportunity to state his

Italians on Mulberry Street. *Courtesy of the Library of Congress.*

admiration regarding the patriotism, industry and progressivism of the people of Italian-Sicilian stock.)

Within a few years of their landing, the criminal elements began to terrorize their fellow immigrants. Various extortion societies, colloquially known as "Black Hand" societies, were in the habit of sending letters written in mockingly deferential tones requesting that their recipient pay up a large sum in cash—or else they and their families would be dust before the end of the week.

The newly arrived immigrants found out that it was better to pay up and be a live coward than a dead hero, and many of them paid the blackmail.

It should be pointed out that the conditions for crime were plentiful at the turn of the twentieth century, owing to the very strange situation at hand. The United States was essentially an immigrant society for most of its history, which meant that waves and waves of new citizens came ashore to the promised land. This meant that unlike in nations such as England, France and Germany (which by the last quarter of the nineteenth century had seen the increase in their populations' peak and did not see anything like the increase found in this country), the

A crowd of Italian Americans on Mulberry Street, a popular spot for immigrants. *Courtesy of the Library of Congress.*

United States was not able to develop the stable local government and legal structures that had appeared in western Europe at a furious rate in this period. The western European nations were able to take a deep breath, look very carefully at their countries and develop the merit-based civil service and local government organization that was one of the most noble features of the developed world.

In the United States, however, the sheer number of immigrants stymied the growth of government reform, since the republic just did not have the time to nurture reforms needed to develop the local apparatus necessary to good government. The only method of dealing with the huge immigration numbers (an estimated one million immigrants per year were coming into the country by the start of World War I, the majority of them Italian Americans) was the "ward boss" system, whereby luminaries such as Boss Tweed and George Washington Plunkett controlled the flow of jobs, housing and money into the districts. The fact that many of the government jobs were filled by election, and not by merit, meant that for decades there was an unholy alliance between the political aspects of government and the technical aspects of government, such as the work of the police and the legal profession. Many police and legal positions were filled with men who were political stooges, which was not something very beneficial either for them as officials or for the department they worked in as a whole.

The position of the Italians was particularly unpleasant. The majority of them came from Naples and Sicily, where the standards of education were very low indeed. Many of them had a great fear of central government, which is not surprising, as the respective rulers of the area treated them abominably. These factors, added to the fact that they often did not speak English, meant that they were at the bottom of the barrel regarding jobs and education. The local Black Hand gangsters, many of whom were connected with the local politicians, found these newcomers—suspicious of outsiders and police, uneducated and demoralized by their new circumstances—to be easy meat. These evil men who prayed on them gave the Italian American community a wholly undeserved reputation as being inherently dishonest.

The growth of the population of the United States, with the accompanying boom in industrial production, brought about with it the inevitable labor-management system.

Chapter 2
THE SYNDICATE
TAKES SHAPE

All of the countries of the developed world became involved in labor-management disputes during the course of their development. Few were associated with the violence found in America at this stage. With trade unions either illegal or powerless in the many of the American states, together with the ferociously pro-business stance of the American government since the end of the Civil War, the lot of labor was a dire one. If workers went on strike, they not only faced the threat of instant dismissal from their jobs but also, if the employers were in a bad mood, the prospect of being shot down by troops called in specifically for that purpose, such as during the great strike at the Pullman Palace Car Company in 1893.

A much quicker way of settling the strike, however, was to call in various local thugs who would assault the labor leaders and drive the strikers back to work. A classic example of this is the great garment workers strike in 1897 in New York, an incident that was the direct cause of one of the most savage and evil of the mob's leaders, Lepke Buchalter, gaining seat on the board of directors of what is commonly now called the Mafia; later Buchalter was literally put in the hot seat, when he was executed in the electric chair in 1944.

The techniques used were very simple. The employers contacted the local gangsters—in this case, one Monk Eastman, who just so happened to be Jewish. Eastman organized his local thugs to "schlamm" the labor leaders, who incidentally also happened to be Jewish, as did a substantial part of the workforce. (Schalmming, for the uninitiated, consists of wrapping a piece of metal pipe in a newspaper and thumping the recipient with it.) The leaders were duly assaulted, and an example was set that would reverberate for decades in America.

The union leaders rapidly realized that they would have to fight fire with fire and, in a move that changed the face of crime in America, went to the local gangsters themselves to ask for protection. So began the catastrophic alliance between labor and organized crime, an event that would leave a terrible stain on the American psyche.

As with schlamming, the methods were simple. The unions took onto their books some gangsters who fought the employer's goons to aid the union.

The results of this were obvious: some of the more perceptive gangsters realized that by controlling the unions they would be able to rip off both the workers and the management. This situation was seen with considerable clarity by the first of the great criminal masterminds of the American republic, Arnold Rothstein, who by agreeing to help the unions with their problems with the employers was able to take money from both and dictate which union got what for its members and which employer stayed in business.

The growth of organized crime into the unions, and the unholy alliance with local politicians, sent America into one of its periodic fits of morality and reform. Reforming presidents such as Theodore Roosevelt ordered the Augean stables of local politics to be cleansed. An attack began on the organized gangs of America before World War I. Some gangs were dissolved. Leaders such as Monk Eastman disappeared to fight in the war; he was decorated for conspicuous bravery and then shot down in 1920 as a result of one of the most ludicrous laws ever passed by an advanced nation.

Chapter 3
PROHIBITION AND THE
BEGINNINGS OF THE MOB

On January 16, 1920, the Volstead Act was passed, which in effect banned the importation, manufacture or selling of alcohol in the United States. Passed by a Congress that bent toward anti-Negro legislation (drink was supposed to take away all restraints from black men, which put innocent white women at risk), and in response to the work of the temperance movement, the imbibing of alcohol was theoretically abolished at this time.

With the possible exception of the United Kingdom joining the European Economic Community, no greater mistake was made by a western power this century; it meant that a law, regarded with derision by almost every logically minded person in the land, was passed that could not be enforced (the Congress that passed the act appropriated very little money to pay the agents who were to enforce it). Overnight, the drinking population of America—which meant most of its adult males and a substantial proportion of its female population—became criminals by indulging in a pastime regarded by all but the most fanatical drys as being harmless.

Prohibition made the gangs, heretofore essentially local bands of thugs, into national criminals. Very quickly the bright sparks among the underworld realized that the smuggling and manufacture of alcohol would bring in huge profits, and many of the men who became the leading criminals of the twentieth century got their first taste of power and wealth by becoming bootleggers: Meyer Lansky, the small Jew from Poland; the Sicilian from Palermo, Charles Luciano, who would be given the nickname "Lucky" after he was kidnapped off the street, tortured, pistol-whipped and left for dead but then survived to become the godfather of crime; Benjamin Siegel, the homicidal New Yorker; and Arthur Flegenheimer, the psychotic killer from the Bronx, better known as Dutch Schultz (and to be known even more as a penny-pinching miser)—all very rapidly joined in the beer smuggling industry, selling their ill-gotten property to illegal speakeasies, the existence of which made every person who went into them a criminal.

The profits from the bootleg liquor industry were so huge that the criminals who got their feet in the door first found that they were making undreamed-of profits. So much money flowed into their hands that they were able to bribe police and politicians on a truly grand scale. In this they were certainly not hindered by the Prohibition agents, who for the most part were a collection of political hacks, or by the then president of the United States, Warren Harding, who allowed the White House to be used as a private saloon.

The state of affairs can be seen by the fact that the erstwhile labor racketeer Monk Eastman, after a distinguished career in the army during the Great War, returned to New York to be given a free pardon for his misdeeds in recognition of his bravery. In 1920, the body of Eastman was found lying in the gutter after a corrupt Prohibition agent, with whom he had been running an illegal bootleg operation, shot him. They are believed to have quarreled over the distinctly important action as to whom would tip the waiter.

The wealth that rolled into the coffers of the criminals was then used to buy protection on a truly heroic scale. Before the coming of Prohibition, the money had been strictly look-the-other-way stuff. The sheer logistical dynamics of bootlegging, however, necessitated money being spent much further up the police and political ladder—and in far greater amounts. The scenario would need men of intelligence and foresight who would be able to see which way the wind was blowing, whom to bribe and how to run a truly national organization. The national idiocy of Prohibition helped to bring about something amounting to national crime. Two men who did not see the value of political contacts would be two of the most famous losers in the history of American crime; their lives would change, in a way they could not have foreseen, the future of American crime: Joe "the Boss" Masseria and Salvatore "the Boss of Bosses" Maranzano.

Masseria had fled from Sicily in 1903 with a murder charge hanging over his head. By 1920, with a combination of luck, ruthlessness and a great deal of treachery, Masseria had managed to make himself the top gangster in New York. In doing so, he had managed to offend some of his younger, more perceptive colleagues, such as Charles Luciano and Frank Costello. Luciano and Costello, with the true open-mindedness that is such a feature of Americanism, were astonished at their boss's old-world hatred of men from mainland Italy and, indeed, from other areas of Sicily.

The young men, having been either brought up in the United States or taken to the republic as young children, realized that honor, in the Sicilian sense, was a ridiculous anachronism, fit only for old men brooding about forgotten wrongs. What mattered first and foremost in America was the greenback, bringing in the dollars. As more than one historian of the mob has pointed out, this was *the* reason for the mob's existence. The more perceptive gangsters regarded Masseria's preaching about honor and not dealing with men from the Italian mainland with incomprehension.

What really shocked the young men of the mob, however, was Masseria's dislike of dealing with politicians. In response to the suggestions that they bribe politicians, so as to make their positions far more secure, Masseria turned down the requests with the (to the younger men, astonishing) statement: "If you get in bed with the politicos, they will corrupt you." To Luciano and Costello, this was absolute rubbish, since they knew full well that the exact opposite was the truth.

The "Young Turks," as they were later called, thought that these notions were utterly ridiculous, even more so when Masseria ordered Luciano to halt his dealings with the brilliant young criminal Meyer Lansky. Lansky, a Jew, was regarded as the brains behind the rackets in New York, where he and his friend, the handsome and savage Benjamin Siegel, would soon run the "Bugsy and Meyer mob," a mob dealing with murder for hire, hijacking liquor shipments and extortion. The viciously anti-Semitic Masseria told Luciano to keep away from Lansky and to put his operations with them in the Masseria pot.

The ruthless and intelligent Lansky realized that this was a signal that Masseria would one day come for him and probably told Luciano, who soon had another beef with his reactionary boss.

The warring gangs of New York, by the beginning of the 1930s, grudgingly accepted the overlordship of Masseria. However, there was a new face on the streets who showed himself to be unwilling to bow a knee to Masseria: Salvatore Maranzano, who in his career was known, albeit very briefly, as "the Boss of Bosses," the only man who would ever hold that title.

Maranzano came from the Castellammarese section of Italy and, by the late 1920s, had managed to recruit a great many followers to his banner. The reasons for his success were many. As a much better-educated man than Masseria (Maranzano was college educated and had been a candidate for the priesthood), he could take a long-term view of affairs; he also realized that the followers of Masseria were getting disenchanted with their leader. It was not only Masseria's refusal to move with the times; it was also the fact—and this was probably the crucial factor—that Masseria was a savagely extortionate leader, demanding huge amounts of tribute from his followers.

Maranzano played on these fears. Masseria—who, though reactionary, was not stupid—realized that he had a fight on his hands.

The years 1928–30 were some of the bloodiest in the history of New York, with at least fifty bodies turning up in various stages of perforation and putrefaction. Luciano, Costello and the rest were bewildered at the ferocity of the exchanges, some of which had to do with the fact that Masseria held it against Maranzano that he came from a different village in Sicily.

At this time, Lansky pointed out the fatuity of the so-called Castellammarese War, which had men being killed (and, more importantly, money lost) in a conflict that satisfied very few. He and Luciano agreed that it would be best to let the two men slug it out with each other until one killed the other—then, of course, they would kill the survivor.

Unfortunately, with bodies dropping at a furious pace, the war did not seem to be coming to an end; Masseria seemed to be willing to let it go on forever.

Luciano and Lansky decided that enough was enough and, it seems, forged a deal with Maranzano. What happened next is one of the most

Meyer Lansky.
Courtesy of the
New York World-
Telegram *and the*
Sun Newspaper
Photograph Collection,
Library of Congress.

famous incidents in the history of the mob in America and is described with considerable accuracy in the book *The Godfather*. Luciano invited Masseria to a sit-down meal at the Nuova Villa Restaurant on Coney Island; among the guests invited was Vito Genovese, who would later make a play to become the Godfather of crime and would spend the last years of his life in a federal slammer, the result of Lansky and Costello framing him on a drug charge.

Masseria seemed to enjoy the lavish meal that his lieutenants had arranged for him, and by 3:00 p.m., he and Luciano were left alone in the restaurant, having a friendly game of cards.

At about 3:30 p.m., Luciano excused himself and went to pay a call to the toilet. It was a most advantageous call of nature, since almost as soon as he had left the table four men came into the restaurant: Benjamin Siegel; Joe Adonis, the handsome bootleg king from Brooklyn; Vito Genovese, who by this action would show how totally treacherous he was, even by mob standards; and the psychotic killer Albert "the Mad

Hatter" Anastasia, who would later be regarded as one of the most evil men in American crime. Masseria looked up and saw the four men aim their pistols at him and died in the hail of bullets.

The four men piled out of the restaurant to a car parked outside. Adonis got into the driver's seat but trembled so much that he could not put the key in the ignition. The ice-cool Siegel contemptuously shoved him out of the driver's seat and drove off. The Castellammarese War was over.

The power that Masseria had used with such foolishness seemed to have had an effect on his funeral, which, by gangland standards, was a hole-in-the-corner affair; even his own wife did not bother to attend. *Sic transit gloria mundi.*

The ramifications of the conflict had an effect on the organization of New York crime, which continues to this day, since Maranzano, with his huge knowledge of Roman history, laid down the administration and structure of the mob.

At a huge meeting of criminals throughout America, held in the Bronx, Maranzano cut out the pieces of the pie for all to see; it would be divided into five families, which is still the way the mob is run today. It was divided as follows:

- The Lucchese family, run by Tommy "Three Finger" Lucchese.
- The Luciano family, run by Charles Luciano, with his underboss Vito Genovese.
- The Profaci family, run by Joe Profaci, with his underboss Joe Magliocco.
- Vincent Mangano, with his underboss Albert Anastasia.
- Joe Bonanno, with his underboss Carmine Galante.

This seemed all well and good until Maranzano, who it appears was the only speaker, made a startling statement: above all of the families would be "the Boss of Bosses," and to no one's surprise, this would be Maranzano himself.

Luciano and Lansky were stunned; they had not gotten rid of one despot—one "Mustache Pete," as the old-style gangsters from Italy and Sicily were contemptuously called—for another, even if Maranzano was more literate than Masseria.

The two young hoodlums kept their feelings to themselves, but within a few months rumors reached them on the gangster grapevine that Maranzano, the embryonic superboss, was having second thoughts about promoting Luciano to his new position.

Maranzano had seen the ferocious ambition that was an integral part of the character of Luciano. Maranzano was also alarmed by the close contact that Luciano had with non-Italian gangs. Unlike Masseria, this did not spring from simple xenophobia but rather from the far more practical realization that by keeping company with Lansky and Siegel, the so-called Kosher-nostra, Luciano was creating a new organization that could threaten him.

Like an Ottoman sultan who plans to kill the assassin who murdered his predecessor, enabling him to claim the throne, Maranzano planned to eliminate this troublesome young upstart.

It appears that not only did Maranzano plan to take out Luciano, but he also decided to take out rather a large number of the Young Turks, including Costello, Siegel, Joe Adonis and the beer baron Dutch Schultz.

One individual who was not on the death list drawn up by the new boss appears to have been Meyer Lansky, the short Jewish mastermind of the mob. This factor is a very important one for anyone wishing to study organized crime in the States; Lansky was the financial and intellectual genius who would lead the mob into the gambling casinos of Cuba, the brains behind creating Las Vegas as the entertainment center of America and the man who would deliberately keep such a low profile that for decades the law enforcement agencies of America—and, indeed, a large number of persons in organized crime—would not have a clue as to his importance.

It was Lansky who probably informed Luciano of the plot to get rid of him and, according to other sources, provided a solution to the problem of Maranzano, the over-mighty ruler.

To solve the problem of hiring a killer to take out a killer, Maranzano hired an Irish gunman, Vincent "Mad Dog" Coll, to solve the Luciano problem. In selecting this twenty-two-year-old killer, Maranzano showed both the ruthlessness and cunning that are the attributes of any good mob boss; being Irish American, Coll was not connected to either the Jewish or the Italian gangs. Coll, therefore, would be able to plan the hit as an

Vincent Coll (middle) leaving homicide court surrounded by police officers. *Courtesy of the New York World-Telegram and the Sun Newspaper Photograph Collection, Library of Congress.*

individual without the tedium of having to ask some of his colleagues to help him. Coll, furthermore, was regarded as a complete pariah among the criminal gangs of New York; a former employee of Dutch Schultz, Coll had complained of the derisory wages that the Dutchman was paying him. (This was a common complaint from anyone dealing with the miserly criminal.) The inevitable shooting war broke out, which ended with Coll's brother being killed and Coll, in a murderous rage, taking out at least four of the Dutchman's gang, as well as, to the horror of both the law-abiding citizens of New York and the mob, killing an innocent five-year-old boy. In hiring Coll, Maranzano had hired the most hated gunman in New York.

With the skill of a pair of urban generals, Luciano and Lansky decided on a counterstrike of breathtaking proportions: they would hire a group of killers who were unknown to "the Boss of Bosses" and kill Maranzano instead.

Lansky and Luciano proceeded to gather a group of Jewish hit men who were unknown to Maranzano. There were, it seems, four of them, including Red Levine, an Orthodox Jew who would not work (kill) on the Sabbath, and Bo Weinberg, a triggerman of Schultz who would, according to some sources, take an unexpected bath on the bottom of the Hudson River, with a concrete pair of swimming trunks for covering, after he betrayed his employer.

On September 10, 1931, the history of organized crime in the United States was changed irrevocably when the telephone call from Maranzano came to Luciano. Could he, together with Costello and Genovese, come to see him at Maranzano's office?

Luciano was only too willing to say that he and his associates would come; the plan regarding Maranzano was put into action.

Soon after the call was made, to Maranzano's surprise, the easygoing Tommy Lucchese called in to see Maranzano. Only a few minutes later, the four killers entered the office of the boss, waving badges that they had been given and claiming that they were Prohibition agents. The guards of Maranzano were lined up against the wall and disarmed. Two of them went into the office of Maranazano, and Lucchese probably identified Maranzano to them. Luciano, with the skill of a street fighter, had used Lucchese as his spy in Maranzano's camp—he had been even before the murder of the boneheaded Masseria.

Maranzano was bemused to see the much-maligned Prohibition agents enter his office. "There is no liquor here," said the erudite boss, probably telling the truth for once.

The answer to this plaintive remark was six thrusts with a dagger by Red Levine. Maranzano—who, like his hero, Julius Caesar, was being killed by the men he had helped create—lunged at the two killers, who promptly shot him four times.

The four assassins promptly decamped from the scene of slaughter, passing on the way downstairs the now redundant assassin Vincent Coll. Apprised of this unexpected turn of events, Coll promptly left the scene as well, $25,000 to the good, the down payment of his fee for dealing with Luciano and the others.

The days following the death of Maranzano were given the title "Night of the Sicilian Vespers" in commemoration of the night in the thirteenth century when the population of Sicily slaughtered the garrisons of French soldiers of the tyrannical Charles of Anjou, whose troops occupied and ravished the land of Sicily. According to Mafia folklore, pro-Luciano supporters, in a blood-purge that strengthened Luciano's hold over the mob, slaughtered a number of Maranzano supporters. According to some reports, more than forty Mustache Petes were killed. More conservative reports note that the number was far fewer. The most interesting figure who was known to have been killed was Gerardo Scarpato, the man who owned the restaurant where Masseria had had his last, opulent meal. Some say that Luciano ordered the hit in order to assuage the remaining Masseria faithful. This author personally believes that Luciano had Scarpato killed because he knew far too much about the treachery of Luciano regarding his old boss, and an embarrassing eyewitness was eliminated.

THE REFORMS OF LUCIANO AND LANSKY: MURDER, INCORPORATED TAKES SHAPE

Like Washington and Jefferson regarding the American colonies after the Revolution, Luciano and Lansky set to work to reform criminal gangs of America. Maranzano's idea, to be a boss of all bosses, was dropped like a hot potato. Luciano was in control of much of the organized crime now, and he was far too intelligent to try to force his colleagues into positions of subordination. A newly styled crime syndicate would now dominate the new mob. This would be a fluid organization that would welcome men from all ethnicities. It would have as its de facto boss the Sicilian-born Luciano. Its members would be the Jewish, Polish-born Lansky; the Italian Joe Doto, who renamed himself Joe Adonis after the handsome Greek hero (Adonis thought that he was a handsome and suave individual, though the pictures of him cast serious doubts on this); Louis Lepke; Arthur Flegenheimer, better known as Dutch Schultz; and Frank Costello. All of these men were based in New York. As a matter of courtesy and practicality, some men from the outlying states were invited: Longy Zwillman, the gang lord of New Jersey, whose death would be one of the most bizarre in the history of the mob; and men from Chicago, such as Jake Guzik, nicknamed "Greasy Thumb" since he handled so much money buying protection from the police and politicians, and Tony Accardo, who proved to be one of the most long-lived of the gang lords of America and, with Lansky, probably the most intelligent.

The rules were quite simple. Each of the gangs would be dominant in a particular area of economic sphere, such as prostitution or gambling. Any disagreements between the various gangs or areas would have to be settled by the syndicate. It would be a remarkably effective way of dealing with disputes, as all of the participants knew the rules, and all knew what would happen if they tried to break them.

At this point, someone came up with the idea of organizing a team of killers that would be responsible for dealing with recalcitrant criminals/businessmen who did not see the error of their ways. Some say that Lansky was responsible for this idea, others say it was Luciano and some say that it was at the behest of Johnny Torrio, the brains behind the Chicago mob of the 1920s. Whatever the reason, the decision was taken to hire a group of killers that would be sent out on contracts handed out by the commission.

The advantages of having an independent team of assassins were all too easy to see. The person set out to be killed would not recognize the man coming to take him out, as he would be a complete stranger to him, unlike the men he had dealt with, whom he could recognize. There would be insulating layers of administrators who would give orders to the assassins at the behest of the syndicate. The most important men at the top would not see the assassins at work and would not give orders to them. They were, in effect, completely cut off from the work of their cohorts, and they would only be in danger if one of the assassins of a high rank informed on them.

The question was, then, where to find them? Not very far away, apparently.

Chapter 4
Kid Twist, Pep and Happy

The area of Brownsville was one of the toughest areas of New York; at the start of the 1930s, the gang of the Shapiro brothers (Meyer, Irving and William) dominated it. They ran the bordellos, terrorized local merchants, dominated the protection rackets and kept an iron grip on the big money industry of the time: slot machines.

Any business that wanted to install vending or slot machines would have to call on the Shapiros, who took an extortionate cut from the profits. Any businesses that did not cooperate could expect to have their premises stink-bombed and their staff, or themselves, thoroughly beaten up.

Like most wise managers, the Shapiros did not dirty their hands with mundane jobs; they hired thugs to do them for them. Two young punks they employed were Abraham Reles and Martin Goldstein. These young men duly did the dirty work for their employers, collecting loans and beating up reluctant businessmen. To their great disgust, however, the Shapiro capo, Meyer, showed no signs of appreciation. He mocked their efforts and refused to promote them to positions of authority. He was particularly sarcastic to Reles. Reles was rather short, looked like a teenager, had a rubbery face and strange, wavy hair and—in a feature noticed by all who met him—had remarkably long arms and huge hands.

Reles and Goldstein felt seething anger for the Shapiros, who were treating them with something akin to contempt. This belief was

Brownsville District, Brooklyn, New York. *Courtesy of the George Grantham Bain Collection, Library of Congress.*

confirmed when Reles was sent to reform school when he was caught doing some dirty work on behalf of Meyer. Reles discovered, to his fury, that the Shapiros were not going to do anything to help him, like get him bail, supply his family with funds or get him a good lawyer. When he emerged into the sunlight on April 1, 1930 (April Fools' Day; someone in authority had a sense of humor, one thinks), Reles vowed revenge on his selfish patrons.

With the help of Goldstein and other rising young punks, Reles ("the Kid" or "Kid Twist," depending on whom you were talking to) proceeded to muscle in on the territory of the Shapiros. Some say that the appellation was due to his youthful appearance, others to a kind of chocolate then extant and others still to the fact that his favorite method of killing was to put his arms around the back of someone's neck and choke the life out of them. He showed himself to be a born leader, leading from the front and always sharing the risks of those under him.

At this point, the Shapiros realized that they had a battle on their hands, and Reles thought that he had an advantage over them: his friendship with a young thug called Joey Silvers. Silvers was employed by the Shapiros in the same way Reles had been. Reles approached him with the suggestion that he tip off Reles and his crew whenever he found the Shapiros alone. One night, his spy told the Kid that the Shapiros were in the vicinity and had their guard down. Reles and company duly arranged an ambush and went to the car in question. Here Reles had his second revelation as to how treacherous the Shapiros could be; within a few seconds gunfire broke out, and Reles found out he had been double-crossed. Silvers, having taken the bribes offered by Reles, had quite casually passed on what had occurred between him and the Kid to the Shapiros. Both Reles and Goldstein were nearly killed in the gunfire, and from now on Reles realized that it was a vendetta.

Things took a turn for the worse, if this was possible, when Meyer Shapiro, seeking the best revenge on the young upstart, decided on an action that, it appears, shocked his own brothers. One day, after seeing Reles's girlfriend walking along the street, he yanked her into his car, beat her into submission, drove her to a secluded spot and then brutally raped her—a sign of "true" male domination and power over a helpless individual. With the wretched young girl lying terrified and demoralized beneath him, he then proceeded to savagely beat her face to a pulp. The gangster, after showing what sort of animal he was, casually shoved her out of the car, telling her to go to the Kid and see what he thought of this display of power.

The Kid nearly went insane with rage at the way his girlfriend had been treated, but with the coldblooded calculation that made him such a terrible foe, he realized that he needed allies to help him overcome the Shapiros.

He approached Harold Maione, a snarling, perpetually scowling gangster who controlled the rackets nearby. Maione, who had been given the sardonic nickname "Happy" by his fellow thugs, was urged into an alliance with the Kid by a sort of gangster mentor, Louis Capone (no relation to the famous gang lord in Chicago), who was a local restaurateur with contacts to the upper echelons of the crime world. It was quickly agreed that an alliance should be arranged between the two young punks, with the Shapiros' territory as the prize.

A band of killers was organized that would soon spread fear through gangland. Besides the Kid and Happy, there was Frank Abbandano, nicknamed the "Dasher." This name came as a result, according to one source, of his skill at running around a baseball triangle while in a reformatory. According to others, it was due to a near-fiasco of a hit when he tried to shoot a longshoreman. The gun in his hand jammed, and the enraged victim promptly chased after him. Abbandano ran so quickly away from this threat that upon circling the block he found himself behind the longshoreman. Upon reaching this decidedly unlucky individual, the Dasher's gun did not jam a second time.

There was also Vito "Chicken Head" Gurino, a hulking thug who honed his skill as a marksman by shooting the heads off chickens.

Then there was Pep. Harold Strauss, a tall, handsome hood, was known as "Big Harry," "Pep" or sometimes "Pittsburgh Phil." This was a strange nickname, as Strauss had never been to Pittsburgh. Pep proved himself to be the most efficient killer the mob had ever known, being thought by some of the more conservative historians of crime to have taken out more than one hundred men. Efficient with a rope, a knife or a gun, Pep proved himself to be one of the main pillars of Reles and the mob, who did not seem to be in any way affected by the day-to-day killings for which he was responsible.

These were among the gang of ruthless sociopaths who Reles assembled one day to tell them of his plan to wipe out the Shapiros.

Blood soon began to soil the streets of Brownsville; Irving went first. On Sheffield Avenue outside of the local Democratic club, the brothers were ambushed by the rebels. A chase through the city streets followed, a veritable urban point to point. Irving thought that he had made it when he managed to get back to one of the apartments where the Shapiros stayed. Instead of safety, he found Reles and Goldstein. Reles shot Irving eighteen times, and the vendetta had started.

Meyer went next, caught by the Kid, the Dasher and Pep. They let the Kid deal with this on his own, and Meyer was probably lucky when the Kid merely shot him through the ear.

The double-crosser was next; Joey Silvers was captured by the Kid, who literally blew his head off.

Willie Shapiro, the last of the brothers, lasted a few more years. His life ended when he was garroted by the Kid in a bar in New York. Pep Strauss, the expert with rope, then tied him up, placed him in a bag and buried him in Canarsie, a district of New York. The body was dug up a few years later, when it was found that the handiwork of the Kid was not so good with this victim, as it showed that there was earth in the man's lungs. He had been buried alive.

So the Kid, Happy and the rest of the crew became the dominant powers in Brownsville. The arrogant young thugs thought that the world was their oyster. It was, because an unexpected bonus would soon fall into their lap.

Louis Capone, the restauranteur with the contacts, had seen the skill by which the young thugs had achieved their objectives. Probably realizing that the syndicate was looking for a bunch of killers, Capone put Reles in contact with the ruling syndicate officials.

Like a young footballer being interviewed by a director of a top club, on March 3, 1933, Reles went to meet the criminal tsar of the unions, Louis Buchalter, better known as Louis Lepke.

In interviewing Reles, Buchalter was following up on the suggestion made that an assassination squad should be formed for the syndicate. Buchalter knew immediately what he was looking for when he saw Reles: a young thug, merciless, intelligent and ambitious. There were other things that the gang lord saw as well. As Reles and his mob were not affiliated with any of the other criminal mobs, there would not be any rivalries that would simmer; they were also ethnically mixed, so no one could complain that a "kike" killed a "wop," or a "dago" took out a "Hebe" and so on.

At this point, it should be stressed—as many writers have done in the past, especially Rich Cohen in his magisterial work *Tough Jews*—how the mob seemed to have been able to work with men and women of a different ethnic mix without any trouble at all. The barriers between the various races of the United States were breached decades before they were "officially" broken down by the legislation of President Lyndon Johnson in the 1960s. As long as the money kept rolling in, and everybody behaved themselves in a reasonable manner, the issue of race did not matter. As many historians of the mob have pointed out, and as Luciano himself repeatedly made clear, the object of the mob was not to kill or terrorize as such—it was to make money. It was this clear ideal of what the mob was there for, and the complete lack of racial tensions (by the standards of the 1930s at any rate), that allowed the mob to progress and develop to its full potential. It should also be pointed out that Luciano was against one of the more ridiculous aspects of organized gangdom: the idea of being made.

Anyone who has seen the huge number of Mafia films that have been produced at a furious pace over the last few years will know that when a man becomes a "made" man of the mob, he will be taken to a darkened room, surrounded by other members of that particular family and probably have his finger pierced by a dagger while some Latin prayer is uttered. This is a sign that the man is now a member of the elect, belonging to an organization that they will leave only when they are dead.

Luciano, a truly open-minded American, had no time at all for this rigmarole, which he probably regarded as childish nonsense. It was at the suggestion of Lansky that he allowed the ceremonies to continue, since it gave many of the new recruits, especially the ones of Italian origins, a sense of belonging to the mob.

Buchalter and Reles soon had an agreement: Reles and his cohorts would be given free hand in their home territories of Brownsville and east New York, while they would be kept on a retainer of $250 per week to deal with any "contracts" the syndicate thought needed attention.

Murder, Inc. was born. Reles and his thugs were now officially recognized as the enforcement arm of the mob, and the higher levels of the syndicate knew that they had the use of an efficient and deadly bunch of killers.

Chapter 5

THE DUTCHMAN GETS SET UP AND THEN GETS OUT

A set of rules is quite all right if all are prepared to obey them. If one member of a corporation decides to go his own way, or to make himself generally obnoxious, the rules tend to get bent. This was the case of Dutch Schultz, the beer baron of New York.

When the syndicate had been set up, there had been a general agreement on which boss was to take what: Luciano took prostitution and vice; Lansky was the financial mastermind; Buchalter took the unions and ripped them off; Costello and Adonis took the political clout; and Schultz was left with the lucrative beer industry and the numbers racket, the American equivalent of the national lottery.

Schultz was not a bedfellow you would recommend; he was a man of gross physical habits, habitually dressed like a slob (Luciano was once heard to complain of him: "The guy has a couple of million bucks and dressed like a pig") and, even among the merciless gang lords of 1930s New York, was looked upon as being a complete psychopath.

Not only was he regarded as being a lunatic, but he also had an even greater drawback in the money-conscious mob: he was regarded as an appalling miser. "You can spit in his face, knock his girlfriend around, and slap his face in public," one observer noted, "but whatever you do, do not try to steal one dollar from him!"

It was this attitude that made the young thug Vincent Coll leave the employ of Schultz in search of new pastures—which proved to be the various rackets of his erstwhile employer. Schultz, enraged at the audacity of the young desperado, forgot his natural penury in going to the forty-second precinct police station in the Bronx and telling the officers that anybody who dealt with the problem of Coll would be suitably rewarded.

The mad young Coll, however, soon found out what it was like to take on the might of organized gangland. On February 9, 1931, Owney Madden, a well-known gangster, was the recipient of a rather abrupt telephone call from Coll, threatening dire retribution if Madden did not come up with a rather large amount of money. Madden had the good sense to keep the Irishman talking while other calls were made to interested parties (the Dutchman).

Coll did get his reward, but not the one he had wanted, since within a few minutes a black limousine was seen parking near the phone booth from which Coll made his call. Three men were seen leaving the car, one of whom took a Thompson machine gun from under his overcoat and calmly shot Coll to death.

The dismissal of Coll and his threats did not seem to bring much joy to the mad Dutchman. In the 1930s, the American republic was in the throes of one of its periodic drives against crime. Its current knight in shining armor was the prosecutor Thomas Dewey, who would twice stand for election as president of the United States. Dewey, a federal prosecutor, had already managed to nail a well-known racketeer, Waxey Gordon, on a tax charge, and the beer baron of New York (whose brew was regarded by the cognoscenti as quite disgusting) was the next in his sights.

For once, the psychotic miser used his head and opened his pocketbook. Faced with a pack of evidence the likes of which had helped bring the mighty Capone down, the lawyers of the Dutchman managed to get the trial of their client moved to Malone, a quiet upstate town in New York State. Within a few days, the Dutchman duly followed. What happened next is a lesson in how a little common sense and a very great deal of money can overturn the dictates of justice. Schultz was seen at local churches, gave to local charities and took part in bingo games and other social events. He also did two things that staggered those who knew him: he gave away a great amount of money, bribing most of the town of Malone, so it seemed, and he very publicly converted to Catholicism. Religion was treated by the mob with indifference, though some seemed to have been genuinely pious. Carlo Gambino, perhaps the only "real" Godfather, died with all the rites of the Catholic Church, while Red Levine, the assassin of Maranzano, never killed on the Sabbath. When the Dutchman, who was born a Jew, converted, his associates were astonished.

Whatever the reasons for the conversion, the money spent and soul transferred seemed to work for the jury; to the unconcealed fury of the judge, the jury, in the teeth of the most cast-iron evidence, found the Dutchman not guilty.

The presiding judge, Frederick Bryant, stormed at the verdict: "The verdict was dictated by other considerations than the evidence." No one bothered to gainsay him.

To the cheers of the crowd, Schultz left the court in triumph and returned to New York to face some very bad news indeed. The indefatigable Dewey, not wasting any time on grieving over the verdict, started attacking Schultz on another front, namely his rackets in the restaurant industry, while the mayor of the city, the ebullient Fiorello La Guardia, was homing in on Schultz's gambling activities. Even worse, the syndicate, with all the instincts of a shoal of piranhas, had been slowly slicing off the pieces of the Dutchman's rackets, thinking, quite logically given the circumstances, that their turbulent partner was not coming back.

Schultz—who had appeared to leave his good sense behind him when he returned to New York, delaying only, according to some observers, to drop his former enforcer, Bo Weinberg (who with more haste than honor had changed sides), at the bottom of the Hudson River in a concrete overcoat—promptly called a meeting of the commission to deal with the Dewey problem. His erstwhile friends came to the meeting with the feeling that they were not going to hear something that appealed to them. They didn't.

Schultz insisted that they use their new murder mob to take out Dewey, the little know-it-all who was set on sending Schultz to the slammer. The syndicate decided, very reluctantly, to see what could be done. Buchalter was given the job of looking at the technical details. In the best of syndicate traditions, he gave the job of checking out the movements of Dewey to one of his most trusted subordinates, Albert Anastasia.

Nicknamed the "Lord High Executioner," Anastasia was, like so many of his ilk, an illegal immigrant from Italy. He soon became a dominant member of the longshoremen's union—the fact that he killed a fellow dockworker did not seem to be held against him, nor did the enforced stay of eighteen months in the death house at Sing Sing prison, from which he was released after four of the main witnesses against him suddenly disappeared without a trace.

Anastasia followed Dewey on his day-to-day routine, using the singularly inappropriate disguise of a father pushing his baby in a pram. The cynical Rich Cohen begs anyone who has a postcard of this coldblooded murderer pushing the little mite around to please send him a copy.

Anastasia, on completion of his mission, reported on Dewey's daily routines, the places he visited and where he could be taken out. Anastasia suggested the deed be done in a local drugstore, where Dewey would go to make a call from a phone booth.

Anastasia said that he could shoot Dewey while he was in the booth, kill his bodyguard and leave. If any civilian got in the way, they could also be dealt with.

If the Dutchman had gotten the idea that his plan would be accepted, he was in for a rude shock. Only the thuggish Gurrah Shapiro (no relation to the Shapiros taken out by Reles and company), the brutal enforcer of Buchalter, seemed to agree with the proposition. The rest of the syndicate, quite rightly, regarded the idea as harebrained—even if it succeeded, it would bring the wrath of all the law enforcement agencies down on their heads.

Schultz, true to form, did not take the rejection gracefully: "You guys stole my rackets, and now you are feeding me to the law. Dewey's gotta go! I'm hitting him myself in forty-eight hours!"

After this outburst, the psychotic miser stormed out of the room. It appears that almost as soon as he had left the room a vote was taken on how to deal with this problem. Of course, the death of the Dutchman was decided. Murder, Inc. would be getting its first big contract.

Three men were tapped for the job on Schultz: Charlie Workman, nicknamed the "Bug," an appellation given to one who was not considered to be altogether right in the head; Emanuel Weiss, a hulking brute of a man, one of the labor goons on the staff of Buchalter; and a third person, known unhelpfully as "Piggy."

The scene was set for one of the most famous executions in gangland history. On October 23, 1935, Schultz was with three of his colleagues: triggermen Abe "Misfit" Landau, "Lulu" Rosencrantz and his gambling wizard Abbadabba Berman, who managed to alter the odds on the various gambling rackets run by the Dutchman so that as little money as possible was paid back to the punters. They were having a business meeting in the Palace Chop House, in Newark, New Jersey, where the Dutchman had to reside as the pressure Dewey was putting on him made it advisable to leave his native state.

At about 10.15 p.m., a car drove up outside the Palace, and three men got out; Piggy, the chauffer, stayed next to the car. Weiss and Workman entered the premises. Schultz and company were in the back room, counting the receipts of the week's business.

Mendy Weiss went up to the barman and waiters and requested them to lay down on the floor. As he was flashing a sawed-off shotgun, everyone saw the logic of his request. Workman casually walked past Weiss and his reluctant audience. There is a little confusion over what happened next. According to one report, Workman breezed up to the men counting the receipts and started shooting. Landau and Rosencrantz fired back, to no avail, dying, with Berman, in a hail of bullets.

Workman then entered the toilet to the back of the tavern, as the Dutchman was nowhere to be seen. Workman then saw a man quietly urinating in one of the urinals. Realizing that this was the mad Dutchman, Workman promptly put a bullet in his back and, staying only to clear out the pockets of the fallen hood, walked away.

According to other reports, Workman first went into the urinals to make sure that no one was hiding there and shot Schultz there and then. At this point, after he had left the urinal, he and Weiss together shot down the gambling genius and the triggermen.

Whatever happened, both Landau and Berman died almost immediately. Schultz, mortally wounded, staggered out of the urinal. His next moments, a veritable dance of death, were recorded by the reluctant owner of the Palace Chop House, Jacob Friedman:

The first thing I noticed was Schultz. He was reeling like he was intoxicated. He had a hard time staying on his pins and he was hanging on to this side. He didn't say a cockeyed thing. He just went over to the table and put his left hand on it, so to steady him. Then he plopped on the chair, just like a drunk would. He said to get a doctor, quick!

Far more interesting were the death throes of Rosencrantz: "When he [the Dutchman] said that, this other guy gets off the floor. He had blood all over him. He throws a quarter on the bar, and says to me get some change for him."

Probably having learned his parsimony from his employer, the gangster waited for some change so he could use the pay phone and not have to pay over the limit. Getting his change, Rosencrantz staggered over to the phone, made the call, demanded the police, collapsed and died.

With the executions over, Workman fled the scene to find no Weiss, no Piggy and no car! Weiss, alarmed at the sound of police sirens, had promptly decamped, leaving the erstwhile assassin on his own.

A furious Workman ran from the place and wandered most of the night thinking of the revenge he would inflict on his treacherous ally. He made his feeling clear at a meeting with Buchalter and Luciano, who managed to calm the hit man down and, as a bonus, sent him on a much-deserved holiday to Miami.

The Dutchman was taken to a hospital and was asked who had shot him. Remaining true to the code of gangland, the Dutchman replied, "I don't know" (which was probably the truth). To the astonishment of the assembled police officers, the Jewish-born Schultz then asked for a priest to confess him.

Toward the end, the police had a stenographer take down the mutterings of the gangster while he slowly left this world.

"There are only ten of us and ten million of them! Please mother, pick me up now…" The Dutchman died shortly afterward. Murder, Inc. had proved its value.

Chapter 6
PEP PROVES HIS WORTH

Of all the assassins used by Murder, Inc. over the next few years, Harry Strauss was the most able. Tall and slim, with a pronounced taste for the good things in life (clothes and women), Harry Strauss, known as "Pep," would become the best hit man in the history of the mob. A man, according to some sources, who would spend an hour a day at his barber getting the best manicure in town, Pep only slept on silk sheets, and whenever he went out to dine, he would invariably select the most expensive dish.

Pep Strauss and the gang had as their headquarters in New York a rather tacky little store at the corner of Saratoga and Livonia Avenues, run by a barely literate woman who, as she ran it almost twenty-four hours a day, was nicknamed "Midnight Rose."

Here the men of Murder, Inc. would stay and gossip. Would the Brooklyn Dodgers have a good season? What is the most efficient technique for murder?

The syndicate lent out their members to other gangs, and given his known efficiency, Pep Strauss was almost always asked to be the hit man during out-of-town jobs.

Like Reles, killing people did not seem to affect Pep one way or the other, and in fact, he was so proud of his skill that he often visited the news agents to pick up the papers of the places he had visited to see the articles written by journalists and to find out the identity of the men he had taken out. Not that he cared one iota over who they were; he just liked to keep in touch with affairs.

Pep was reported to have killed more than one hundred men—some say that the figure is over three hundred—and managed to kill more than twenty men in Brooklyn itself.

Pep was very inventive in his techniques of murder, being able to use a gun, a knife or a rope—the last article, as will be seen, was his specialty. He had the ability, like all good professionals, to blend into his surroundings, which can be seen by his taking out of an old gangster living in Florida who could not speak a word of English.

Pep was shown the target by the local crew and became acquainted with him. To show his credentials, Pep opened his suitcase and proceeded to show the individual in question his arsenal of weapons. By sign language—murder being, like other things, an international trade—Pep showed him that he was an assassin. The target promptly grasped Pep's intention and showed him a place where the murder could take place, taking the rope in his hands, as this would be the best means of termination. Pep thanked the man, strangled him and promptly went home.

Another contract Pep carried out, which shows the admiration he evoked among his peers, was regarding a wild individual, Harry Millman, the only surviving member of the "Purple Gang," a group of mobsters who had, like so many of their peers, become rich on the proceeds of bootleg liquor they smuggled over the Great Lakes to an appreciative American public.

A combination of gang warfare and police action had reduced their ranks until the only one of the gang still in circulation was Harry Millman, who had been reduced to the level of shaking down the local brothels and trying to carry on the local extortion rackets.

As author Robert Rockaway dryly points out, by this stage "Millman was more a Hooligan than a Hoodlum," but he must have offended somebody—he survived an attempt to kill him after a bomb was placed in his car. Unfortunately for the assassin, Millman was attending a nightclub at the time, and it was the club doorman who was asked to drive the car away. The doorman was duly blown to bits, and the powers that be in the underworld decided to bring in professionals.

Enter Pep Strauss and his fellow Murder, Inc. member, Happy Maione. Millman, through the whisky-soaked mists that were affecting his mind, realized that he was now in danger and only walked about in crowds when he left his house. This, of course, presented no danger to Happy and Pep.

In November 1937, at the delicatessen Boesky's on Hazelwood and Twelfth Street, Millman must have thought that he was safe, as he was dining out among a crowd of people. No one in his right mind would try to take him out in such a crowded place.

This is where Murder, Inc. proved its worth. While eating, two men approached Millman; they must have made quite a sight, as Pep was tall and lean and Happy short and stout. Oblivious to the mayhem they could cause, Pep and Happy opened up on their hapless victim. Nine slugs went into the body of the unfortunate Millman, lead from a gun being more efficient than a blast from a bomb, at least in this case. Millman expired (promptly, one thinks), while four innocent diners were wounded in the shootout. Pep and Happy casually stalked out, leaving the rest of the diners in a state of pandemonium.

One contract that Pep could not fulfill has gone down in gangland history: the axe murder that wasn't. Pep had been sent down to Florida (again) to take out a victim. He followed the man around but was not able to find a location that would enable him to carry out his professional duties.

His pride hurt, Pep followed the man until he came to a movie theater. The man sat down, closely followed by Pep. How to do the job—a gun would be far too noisy.

The eye of the assassin fell on a fire axe in the corner. It was to be used in case of an emergency. Well, thought the handsome killer, wasn't this an emergency? He would get the axe, put it through the head of the victim and then make his exit.

Pep grabbed the axe and resumed his position—only to find that the victim had changed his place! Pep thought that the job was under a curse and stormed back to Brooklyn. This is the only contract that Pep is known to have failed. Usually, he and his associates were expert practitioners of their art, especially among their own.

Among the mob, like other bureaucracies—the civil service, the army and the police—the group is regarded as being more important than the elements that make it up. Stealing from it is regarded as one of the cardinal offenses of the mob. Such is the case of Walter Sage, who had been given the job of looking over the slot machine operation of the mob on Long Island.

Sage was known as one of the gang; he had once roomed with Pep and another Murder, Inc. desperado, Gangy Cohen. Unfortunately, after a while, it was noticed that Sage's books did not balance. As Rich Cohen pointed out, in the mob, one bad deed wipes out all of the good works. Despite the fact that he had lived with Pep and Cohen, Sage had to go. And who better to show him the error of his way than his erstwhile partners.

The mob often uses the best friend of the accused to take him out. This is for two reasons: it is a test to see if the man selected for the role of executioner will carry out the deed. It is, in effect, a brutal test of loyalty, one that very much resembles the habit of the English king Henry VIII, who put family members of the accused in the jury to test their loyalty to him, or of the Soviet dictator Joseph Stalin, who in the great army purges of the late 1930s put the leading marshals of Russia on trial and had their fellow officers command the firing squad that killed them. The second reason is far more down-to-earth: who is going to suspect that your best friend is going to kill you? "Et tu Brutus," Caesar is said to have murmured when he was killed in the senate. Exactly the same words could be said by legions of gangsters who realized at the last minute they had been betrayed.

Sage had stolen, and so Sage had to go. He went in true Murder, Inc. style.

Many of the syndicate, Sage among them, were on holiday in upstate New York. Sage was invited for a midnight ride with friend Cohen. As they drove, Pep and other Murder, Inc. men followed closely behind. By the lights of their headlamps, they were able to see what happened next. Cohen, who was sitting behind Sage, leaned forward and drove an ice pick (a favorite weapon of the boys) into the embezzler's body. Sage screamed and the car went out of control, while Cohen hung onto his friend's neck and stabbed him more than ten times.

The car, not surprisingly, ended up in the ditch, and the rest of the team came out to view Cohen's handiwork. To their astonishment, Cohen promptly bolted for the trees and disappeared into the night.

Leaving their absent friend to his own devices, Pep and company proceeded to take Sage's corpse to a nearby lake. His body was tied to a pinball machine (a nice touch for a man whose death had been caused by embezzling the accounts of these money makers), and then, presumably just to make sure that he was dead, Pep drove an ice pick into the wretched cadaver thirty-two times. The body was then dumped in the lake.

One small detail escaped the attention of the lean, handsome hood: the natural gases that were found in the decomposing body floated it to the surface. Pep had forgotten to perforate the stomach and the bowels. "How about that," Pep observed, "you have got to be a doctor with this bum or he floats!"

An interesting fact about this particular death was the destiny of Gangy Cohen. Probably realizing that he could be next on the list of his colleagues, the reluctant killer fled the scene to the nearest railway station. Cohen traveled across the whole of the American continent, finding his way to California. Here, owing to the contacts he had with his "associates," he got a job as a movie extra, acting under the pseudonym Jack Gordon; he made a name for himself playing, of all parts, policemen.

If stealing from the mob was bad enough, talking to the police was even worse, which is why Whitey Rudnick had to go. A heroin addict, Rudnick was seen talking to a member of Dewey's staff.

To be seen talking to a cop or a prosecutor, not altogether surprisingly, caused great suspicion among the syndicate. Buchalter, the boss of the industrial scams and the de facto head of Murder, Inc., gave the signal to terminate Rudnick.

What made the contract on Rudnick so interesting, however, was the cunning manner in which the syndicate went about it. A lesson, a very public one, had to be given to men who tried to inform on their colleagues. It was decided that a note be dropped in the pocket of the informer so it would be discovered by the police, who would then know that the syndicate had discovered that Rudnick was a rat.

The semiliterate Strauss and Reles typed the letter, with some difficulty. The letter is shown here, in its entirety, to show the brilliant manner in which the hoods thought they could pull one over on the police.

Friend George

Will you please meet me in NY some day in reference to what you told me last week? Also I have that certain powder that I promised you the last time I seen you. PS I hope you found this in your letter box sealed. I remain your friend. YOU KNOW, FROM DEWEY'S, THE DISTRICT ATTORNEY'S OFFICE.

With the letter typed, the contract was handed out to Pep Strauss. They decided to deal with Rudnick by taking him to Happy Maione's garage in the Ocean Hill area of New York. When asked later if that was all they had planned, Reles replied quite casually, "We didn't need any other plan; we are experts."

Rudnick, the drug addict, was spotted by the gang on the night of May 4, 1937. He was not too far gone in the morphine haze to know that seeing the gang of killers looking for him was not good news. He promptly went off in the other direction, with Dasher Abbandando in hot pursuit. Rudnick was soon bundled into a car and taken to Happy's garage. By a macabre coincidence, Maione's own grandfather was living in an apartment opposite and was being attended by grieving relatives as he was dying.

Reles drove to the garage, where he found Pep, Happy and Dasher in characteristic poses: Dasher was pinning the would-be rat to the floor and Pep, the expert with the rope, was tying a knot around Rudnick's neck, while Happy was holding a meat cleaver.

"We don't need you," remarked the latter. "The work is all over."

Happy wiped his hands. "You wouldn't think that such a skinny bum would put up such a fight."

The gang proceeded to put the body of Rudnick in a stolen car. While folding him up and putting him on the back seat, the "corpse" let out a groan. "This goddamn bum ain't dead yet!" yelled Pep, who reached for the ice pick and punctured the body a few times. "That oughta finish the bum," remarked the assassin.

Following the usual routine, the body was taken in the stolen car to a residential street in New York. Happy Maione put the letter into a pocket of the corpse.

When the gang got back to the garage, Happy was given the sad news that his grandfather had died. Happy, though, was delighted. He had an alibi regarding the murder. How could he have killed someone when he was at his grandfather's deathbed?

Or so he thought.

Chapter 7
ENTER DEWEY, EXIT LUCIANO

While Murder, Inc. was establishing its credentials, the great Luciano was about to receive a rather unpleasant shock.

Dewey, the man he had saved from the guns of the Dutchman, was appointed by the governor of New York, H. Lehman, to be the special prosecutor on organized crime. The first man in the sights of the prosecutor was Luciano.

Knowing that parts of the New York Police Department were extremely corrupt, he proceeded to hire his own investigators, soundproof his office and adopt a new plan of campaign: instead of taking in the mobsters one at a time, he would pull them in bulk, so no one would be able to inform his colleagues what was occurring. So it was on January 31, 1936, at 8:00 p.m. that the call girls and madams of New York were brought in for questioning. Hookers with such gracious names as Polack Francis, Sadie the Chink and Jennie the Factory were hauled in and questioned.

The name of "Mr. Ross" came up time and again. Mr. Ross lived in the Waldorf Astoria Hotel. So, interestingly, did Luciano. Mr. Ross apparently had a great taste for showgirls. Some of them even described what his apartment looked like.

Mr. Ross appeared to control the hookers and their pimps. Luciano, reading the writing on the wall, made tracks to the criminal-friendly resort of Hot Springs, Arkansas, run by fellow mobster Owney Madden.

Luciano spent a fortune trying to pay off the local police and politicians, all to no avail, since in the autumn of that year Luciano was hauled back up to New York and charged with being associated with the prostitution industry.

The headlines of New York papers were jammed with details of the sins of the Mafia boss. Some of the call girls brought in to give evidence spoke very disparagingly of Luciano's sexual performance, something that, according to some onlookers, enraged Luciano as nothing else did.

Luciano went on the stand and, like most gangsters, made a fool of himself. The underworld said that Lucky had been given a bad trial and that many of the witnesses were bribed. This may have been so, but the jury, and history itself, thought and thinks otherwise. Luciano was found guilty on sixty-two counts of white slavery. Judge Philip McCook, the presiding judge, remarked, "You are one of the most vicious criminals that has ever been brought before this court. It is the sentence of this court that you serve thirty to fifty years."

The founder of the modern Mafia, sent to prison by the man whose life he had saved, was taken away from the court, with the cameras of the reporters of the various newspapers recording every step, the light bulbs flashing like a battalion of searchlights in a blitz.

Luciano was taken to be housed in the state penitentiary at Dannemora, near the Canadian border, one of the toughest prisons in America. It was here discovered that the gang lord was suffering from venereal disease and was a morphine addict.

The newspapers trumpeted the fact that the most powerful criminal in America had been thrown in the slammer. Others surely would follow.

MURDER, INC. IS DISINCORPORATED

The imprisonment of Luciano, to begin with, did not do much to harm the mob. Like a king in waiting, Lucky, even from behind the walls of his prison, was kept well informed of the affairs of his creation. He managed to give orders and manage decisions taken and murders organized, the usual tasks of the CEO of the goon squad.

Lucky, however, may have counted himself fortunate to be in his present predicament, since the hit squad he had helped organize was about to come apart at the seams, the result of one of the most infamous episodes in the history of the American republic: the confessions of Abraham Reles, a founding member of Murder, Inc.

It started in January 1940 when, in yet another move against criminals, Reles was hauled up on a vagrancy charge and promptly thrown into the slammer nicknamed "the Tombs." Presumably to keep him company, Happy Maione was also arrested at the same time, and the Tombs found itself the happy recipient of two of the most notorious killers in America. All that the twosome of death would have to do, as they had done so often in the past, was to keep their mouths shut and open their pockets, and after a brief incarceration, they would be free to embark on the trade of slaying.

Then Harry Rudolph appeared. Rudolph was a small-time crook who was currently taking a holiday, courtesy of the federal government, in the city workhouse for various unimportant crimes. Only a few days after Reles was arrested, the district attorney's office was surprised to receive a note from him, informing them that he had information about a murder committed in 1933, the part of the main character of this incident being filled, reluctantly one feels, by Red Alpert.

According to Rudolph, Alpert was a small-time hood, with a hatred for the police (not a very strange feeling for some of the characters in this book). Alpert had lately, and dishonestly, acquired rather a splendid set of diamonds. Knowing Pep Strauss, and knowing that he was fairly flush with funds, he offered them to the handsome hood, the Beau Brummell of the syndicate, for the knock-down price of $3,000.

Pep showed his arrogance by offering $700, an offer that Alpert correctly concluded as being an insult but incorrectly showed it by telling Pep to go to hell. A furious Strauss promptly set about planning the termination of this upstart for his impertinence but, for once, was held back by Reles, who could not see the point in this particular whack.

Reles went over to see Alpert with the chunky Martin "Buggsy Goldstein," the syndicate clown. After explaining to Alpert the folly of his words, they made a counteroffer for the diamonds: $700. Alpert told them they could go to hell. It was a foolish man who insulted the most able hit man in the history of the republic. It was even worse when a trio of killers was insulted. Alpert had to go.

At this point, a classic Mafia ploy took place. As Alpert knew by sight the trio of killers, he would be very suspicious of them if they now approached him again. The problem of how to get rid of Alpert lay in getting him to let his guard down.

At this point, Walter Sage made his entry—before he made his exit, courtesy of Pep and company. Sage was a friend of Alpert, so Pep decreed that Sage was to lure Alpert into a position where his impertinence could be dealt with in a rather abrupt manner.

Alpert was a friend, but business is business, as Sage must have realized. He contacted Alpert, and the result was that a rather interesting piece of information was put on a list of unsolved murders in the police records: "Alpert. Alex, alias Red. 19 Years of age. Small-time hoodlum. Shot at the edge of a yard. Nov. 25, 1953. No witnesses." (Surprise, surprise.)

Rudolph was a friend of Alpert's and accused Reles and Goldstein of having killed him. The wheels were set turning of what was to be the most sensational gangland betrayal until the days of Joseph Valachi, Sammy Gravano and Donnie Brasco.

Why Rudolph was willing to confess, over six years after the event, has puzzled historians for decades. A statement of murder, however, is a statement of murder. As a result of Rudolph's statement, the police started investigating this affair again and also, compliments of Rudolph again, picked up two criminals attached to the syndicate: Dukey Maffeatore and Pretty Levine.

The two of them were rapidly made aware of the truism that there is no honor among thieves, and even less among hit men, when they found out that a bail bondsman had offered $5,000 to anyone who offered to let Maffeatore take the blame for the Alpert killing.

Slowly but surely, the two men began to become aware they were being set up. They both began to talk about what they knew.

On March 21, Reles was visited by his attorney in the Tombs. What transpired between them will never be known, but after the visit he wrote to his wife asking her to request a meeting with the district attorney.

A meeting was arranged with Burton Turkus—the attorney in charge of dealing with mob affairs, whose book on the running of Murder, Inc. is invaluable to anyone wishing to study how the mob operated in the early days—and William O'Dwyer, the district attorney.

A deadly game of bluff and counter-bluff began between the establishment figure and the hood. Reles showed a staggering grasp of the law, together with a nonchalance that verged on arrogance, which made the attorneys want to smack him in the jaw. Reles jeeringly stated that with the very little they had on him, no jury in the world would be able to convict him. Correct.

Reles claimed that he would be able to make a complete idiot of anyone on their own who tried to accuse him of murder. Correct.

Reles told the attorneys that if he was able to walk out completely clean, he would give them information that would shatter the organization he worked for, *but only if he was able to walk out clean.* Problem.

Should the government let a man who had killed a score of men give evidence and then walk away from the affair a completely free man? Reluctantly, they agreed.

Reles started to talk…and talk…and talk. To the astonishment of the attorneys and the stenographers who took down his confessions, Reles seemed to have a photographic memory. He reeled off facts and figures, dates and details of murders and conversations years old. His confession led to information on the killing of eighty-five people in Brooklyn alone; his statements filled seventy-five notebooks.

The news that Reles was ratting to the police sent shock waves through the underworld. Men began to run for cover; others sought to kill parties who could confirm what the Kid had said. Why did Reles confess when the evidence against him was rather thin?

Some say that he was becoming distressed about the way his wife and family were suffering. Many police officers scoffed at this, as Reles had never shown any feeling when his son came home weeping after being told by his schoolmates his father was a murderer.

There was a rumor that he was getting tired of the life of crime and that his conscience was affecting him. Once again, the police scoffed.

There is another story, one that rings true to this author. Reles, being a very cool and clever man, knew that he was in a ship that was about to sink. There were already rumors that the powers that be in gangland wanted Murder, Inc. to be terminated. This would mean a few hit men going on welfare, knowing rather a lot about how the syndicate operated. Having both a worm's-eye and bird's-eye view of knowledge as to how the syndicate dealt with those they felt to be disaffected or weak, Reles had a fairly good idea that he had better get his blow in first, or he would be just another corpse in an alleyway.

"I am not a stool pigeon" Reles repeatedly affirmed. "Every one of the other guys would have hung me if they could." He was probably right.

In the next few weeks, arrests were made throughout New York. Some, like Albert Tannenbaum, another killer in the stable of Murder, Inc., and Vito "Chicken Head" Gurino, became informants themselves. The results of the confessions of Reles and company ended with both Happy Maione and Frank Abbandando being hauled up for the murder of Whitey Rudnick. (Pep Strauss was also considered for this murder, but spoiled for choice, the authorities had both him and Buggsy Goldstein arrested for the murder of "Puggy" Feinstein much later.)

Reles himself was taken to a number of secure locations, never fewer than six officers guarding him, while someone was in the same room as him whenever he went to bed at night.

On May 13, 1940, while in Europe the old democratic order would soon come crashing down, Happy Maione and Frank Abbandando walked into the courtroom of Judge Franklin W. Taylor.

The fact that the police took this case seriously can be seen by the fact that twenty patrolmen guarded the corridors, while twenty detectives ringed the courtroom. Sharpshooters were put on the windows and doors of the courtroom, while other detectives sat unobtrusively in the courtroom itself.

The two men gleamed with sartorial elegance—Maione dressed in a blue serge suit and two-tone tie and Abbandando in a blue suit and flaming red tie. As with the other members of the mob, they had the best lawyers money could buy.

At 10:00 a.m., Burton Turkus, the slim and debonair district attorney, led off for the prosecution. He called more than fourteen witnesses regarding the death of Rudnick, stating how the former stool pigeon had died with sixty-three stab wounds and a shattered skull. He described the note found in the dead man's pocket.

Then the informants began to appear, beginning with Dukey Maffeatore, who must now have realized what he had gotten himself into. He described how he had clipped a car (the judge, an establishment figure if ever there was one, had to be told that this meant the car was stolen) and how Pep Strauss was furious when he heard that the car had not been stolen from out of the neighborhood.

Then Reles appeared. The prosecution had brought out its ace in the hole. Maione and Abbandando stared in horror as the Kid cheerfully began to relate the truth of Murder, Inc.

Reles had changed shape since his enforced incarceration: lack of exercise meant that he had become pudgy, and his odd way of walking, as if he was kicking a football in a phone booth, was reduced to a shuffle. The evidence he gave, however, rocked the court. For six hours he was on the stand, explaining the techniques of murder. Despite all the defense could do to him, even bringing up the rape of his girlfriend, he answered the questions he was given coolly and accurately. When the Kid described how he had aided in the assassination of the stool pigeon, the fact that Rudnick had been a friend of his for more than fifteen years did not appear to faze him in the slightest. He managed to convey the brutality of the murder, as well as the individual efforts of all concerned: Pep Strauss, using the ice pick to perforate the body of Rudnick; Maione, hitting the wretch with a cleaver "just for luck"; the Dasher, buckling up the body to make sure it fitted in the car. As the final layer of icing on the cake, the Kid explained how when he and Happy had been in the Tombs prison, they had attended a religious service, though he did not appear to know what sort of religion the service was all about.

The court listened to this epiphany with a startled silence. When informed of the religious service, the judge dryly reported that if Reles had known which particular religious service he was attending, "it didn't do him much good!"

The defense team was let loose on him—and rapidly wished they hadn't been. Reles, with the biting, arrogant nastiness that Turkus had casually mentioned was all too typical of him, proceeded to catch the defense in errors of fact. He pointed out to one embarrassed counsel that when the Dasher was in prison, he was kept in the penitentiary at Attica, not Elmira, and that he had visited him there. He told them of the murders he had committed and of how Maione had been in a car when he had driven the corpse away for disposal.

The defense was left reeling with this statement, something that did not go down very well with Maione, who showed his annoyance with Reles at the adjournment for the court for the day. While being led away from the court, Reles met on the way to the cells his old, surly partner, Happy Maione, all five foot, four inches of him. The runty assassin lunged for the Kid, shouting, "You stool pigeon son of a bitch! I'm gonna tear your throat out!"

For several seconds, the two killers were kept apart only by the efforts of their guards. It is reported that the eyes of the pint-sized killer bulged with hate as he tried to get his treacherous partner. The courtroom had a fine view of friendship, Murder, Inc. style.

When Maione took the stand in his own defense, he had up his sleeve an alibi that many thought to be perfect. The night the syndicate terminated Rudnick, one of Maione's relatives, Grandfather Selenga, had died. In true Italian fashion, the family had been at the bedside. They all swore that Happy had been with them and that (of course) he had been Grandfather Selenga's favorite grandson.

This dutiful grandson had been in the house from 9:00 p.m. to 9:00 a.m.—hours, the reader may observe, when Rudnick was being stabbed, strangled, pickaxed and cleavered. How could the runty little killer be taking out Rudnick when he was at his grandfather's bedside?

If Happy and the Dasher were pleased with the evidence given, they could only be forgiven for being so. This feeling must have quickly dissolved when the prosecution called a certain witness—the undertaker who had dealt with the body of Grandfather Selenga.

Mr. Nicholas Blanda was the neighborhood undertaker who, as it happened, had buried Happy's father. And his grandfather, too. It should be pointed out that in the trade followed by Happy undertakers were not the sort of individuals you called on to help you with your job.

Mr. Blanda, a dignified and calm man, explained how he had been called on the morning of May 25 to attend the body of Grandfather Selenga. He and, for that matter, the embalmer who came with him had stated that they had prepared the body that morning and that they had not seen Happy at all.

The defense team, thrown considerably out of sync with this statement, was reduced to asking questions that verged on the bizarre, which as any lawyer will tell you is a sure way of putting your client behind bars.

"Is it true," said one of the defense team, in a desperate attempt to destroy the credibility of Blanda, "that you have a horror of touching bodies and that you yourself never touch a body?"

"I, sir, have been an undertaker for over twenty years!" came the crushing reply, which probably, in the jury's mind, sent Happy to the chair.

The Dasher, Abbandando, was questioned next and, unlike Happy, called no witnesses except for himself. This would not do him any favors.

It appears that the seriousness of the proceedings had not entered into the Dasher's psyche, since he seemed to be more concerned that, by being there, he would not be able to attend the first night ball game of the season. He did not appear to have any feelings for his wife and family, already on relief.

The Dasher gave out his evidence in a mixture of sneering contempt and a bellow. Accused of raping a girl, he said that it did not matter, as he had married her. No, he had not killed anybody; he could not have killed Rudnick, as he had never worked in a garage; no, he could not remember where he was on the night Rudnick was killed; no, he had never heard of Albert Anastasia; and no, he did not dispose of the car in which Rudnick had been killed.

If these flat denials did not do any good to the Dasher, what happened next was even worse. It was revealed that in 1928 he and Happy had helped two other thugs beat up policemen. At the trial that followed, he had been found guilty of assault and had been sent to the slammer.

"My lawyer was not there the whole trial, I was forced to trial by the judge!" he said. Problem: the judge who was dealing with the case at hand had also dealt with the case in 1928. It is very foolish to insult a judge in his own court.

"This court never prosecutes an accused without counsel being present," a rather indignant Judge Taylor retorted. "Walter Hart represented you!"

"The court's statement is not an accurate one," the lawyer of Abbandando foolishly remarked.

"Counsel is disorderly!" replied the outraged judge.

At this point, the Dasher uttered a threat to the judge in a low voice, as if the judge was a customer falling behind on the debts he owed. What was said is not known, but the judge wisely ordered a court officer to stand between him and the powerfully built villain. This outburst could not be said to have done the Dasher much good. Abbandando could be forgiven if he could now see the straps pulled down over him in the chair.

The final arguments were made to the court. The lack of sustenance to the position of Abbandando can be seen by the fact that his lawyer was reduced to remarking on the sporting skill of his client: "Ballplayers don't kill people. In all my experience I cannot think of a single baseball player who ever killed anybody."

If this particular revelation did not help the defense, what happened next helped them even less. While Turkus was addressing the court, Maione growled, "Reles told you everything!"

The whole of the court looked at the runty killer glaring at Turkus. The pint-sized hit man had finally, it seems, realized what sort of position he was in. Abbandando, who had for so long been the poodle to Maione's master, stared in disbelief at the way his boss appeared to have collapsed.

"Reles told you everything!" Maione screamed at the startled attorney. As this is what the Kid had been doing for days, the logic of

Sing Sing prison. *Courtesy of the George Grantham Bain Collection, Library of Congress.*

the statement was irrefutable. It could not have helped him when the jury was sent out to consider its verdict. Despite the evidence, the two men seemed to be quite confident of, if not beating the rap, at least not being sent to the chair.

On May 23, 1940, after only two hours of deliberations, the jury came back. Guilty.

On May 27, the dainty killer, Maione, and his oafish sidekick listened to the court verbiage that essentially meant they were going to be fried in the chair.

The following day, the two assassins were put on the train that would send them up the river to Sing Sing prison—and to their appointment with justice. It seems that here it hit them that they were going to be strapped in the chair and sent to their gods. They tried to duck the flashbulbs of the cameramen who attended their journey. One of the newsmen had the bright idea of asking Maione—who was an expert in such matters—of the city's attempt to reduce crime. After having stated that he thought it was a good idea, Maione added a rider that he had never seen Reles in his life.

The newsmen and women must have laughed when they heard that.

Chapter 8
Pep and Buggsy

On September 9, 1940, the towering Pep Strauss and the jovial Buggsy Goldstein went on trial for the murder of Puggy Feinstein. There was quite enough evidence for Pep Strauss to have been charged with the murder of Rudnick, but a rather odd incident had stymied this. And it was all to do with women.

Evelyn Mittleman was a very attractive woman who made a habit of hanging around gangsters, some of whom seemed to die rather young. Pep Strauss took a fancy to her, apparently bumping off a previous lover, and in true gangland style, he bought her expensive gifts, including diamonds, which Ms. Mittleman loved to show off. The year 1940 found her, however, in the women's house of detention, as a witness against her lover. She advised Pep to inform on his associates, as had Reles. Pep agreed, under the condition that he walk out clean and that he could see Reles on his own.

The sight of the premier hit man in the mob's history walking free was too much for anyone to bear, and the lean hood was told that his offer was not accepted. The request to see Reles was also turned down, since in the mood Pep was in, murder would have certainly followed.

So it was that the lean killer took his place in the courtroom with the clown of the group for the murder of Puggy Feinstein, whose death shows just how much the mob values its own territory.

Puggy Feinstein, whose real first name was Irving, was discovered on a night in 1939. He had gotten his nickname owing to the flattened state of his nose, compliments of an unsuccessful career as a boxer. He had been a petty crook but was now trying to go straight and, after working in a factory, had set himself up as a gambler in Borough Park. Problem: this particular piece of turf belonged to Vince Mangano, an acquaintance of Albert Anastasia.

There is no nonsense in the mob about healthy competition—what you have you hold. Mangano was not happy with this competition. He made his feelings known to Anastasia, who made them known to Murder, Inc. Puggy had to go.

The manner by which Puggy went horrified even hardened police officers of the time. Puggy owed some money to a local loan shark in Brownsville and visited the area to pay the debt off. His whereabouts were rapidly brought to the attention of Pep and company, who decided to take Puggy out at the earliest opportunity. Having been told that the unfortunate ex-boxer would be back the next day, Reles, Pep and Buggsy decided to lure Puggy into a car (stolen, compliments of Maffeatore, of course), take him to Reles's house and finish him off there.

"My house!?" remarked Reles.

"What's the difference," said Pep Strauss, who had suggested this location. "I don't make any noise, and when I mug them they stay mugged." Reles, of all people, knew that this was the truth.

Puggy was duly lured into a car and brought to Reles's house. What happened next is best described in the words of Reles and Maffeatore, who, against the strict orders of Pep Strauss, accompanied the trio of the Kid, Pep and Buggsy into the spider's parlor. Reles, on entering his house, discovered present both his wife and that of Goldstein, who he thought had gone to the movies together. Reles gave his wife fifty dollars and told the pair of them to leave and find something to do. Reles's mother was sleeping in another room, but this did not stop him from doing what he did next.

"As soon as Puggy passes the chair, Harry jumps up and passes his arm round him [Puggy], mugs him like this." Here the Kid, eyes glinting, stood up in the witness box, showing how you curled an arm around the neck of a victim.

Puggy wriggles around and fights, and shouts, "Don't hit me, I've got the money." I put the radio on a little louder, because Puggy is making a noise. I go for the rope. I go back to the couch with it, and Harry is saying, "The bastard bit me in the hand." Harry is like laying over Puggy so he cannot move. Buggsy is hitting him to keep him quiet.

I give Harry one end of the rope, and I hold the other end. Puggy is kicking and fighting. He is forcing his head down so we can't get the rope under his throat. Buggsy holds his head up, so we can put the rope under. Then me and Harry exchange the ends…cross them, so we can make a knot, a twist. Then we cross them once more. Then we rope around his throat again, to make two loops.

Buggsy gets Puggy by the feet and me and Harry get him by the head. We put him down on the floor. He is kicking. Harry starts tying him up. I am turning him like, and Harry gets his feet tied up with the back of his neck. He ties him up like a little ball. His head is pushed against his chest. His head is folded up against his chest. His hands are in between. The rope is around his neck and under his throat. If he moves the rope will tighten up around his throat more.

The courts listened in horror to the story. They listened as the Kid told them how Puggy strangled himself to death, defecating on the floor of the room as he did so. Dukey Monteafore watched with astonishment at this example of Pep's handiwork.

Pep, enraged that a victim fought back, gave the corpse a kick. "That bastard could give me lockjaw!" the lean killer shouted.

Reles put some lotion on the injured hand. While this was going on, Buggsy managed to get a can of gasoline. The body was taken to the car, and Buggsy and the presumably reluctant Dukey took it to an abandoned dump, poured petrol over it and lit it up.

Unfortunately, Buggsy's skill as a killer did not match his skill as a cremationist. The feet were not cremated, and some rings were able to be taken from the corpse when the police discovered it a few hours later.

The body was identified by the brother of the dead man, who just happened to be a clerk in the law department of the city of New York. Strangely enough, a lawyer, S. Levy, wrote to a local newspaper an article regarding the life of Puggy:

Dear Sir

I desire to write a few words concerning Puggy Feinstein.

Puggy and I played punchball together; he was a small fellow who wished to be a big shot. So, we took different paths. But both paths are so closely entwined, that we should understand those who take a path we just miss. He, too had a fine background.

Last year Puggy told me how he was going straight, he had fallen in love with a respectable flatbush girl. But after he bought the furniture and planned the wedding, a neighborhood boy went up to his folks and told them of his past. They broke up the match and broke his heart.

He reverted to type.

He was a swell punchball player.

Farewell Puggy Feinstein

Dukey, unnerved by the firsthand view of the Murder, Inc. technique, got lost on his way back to Brownsville. He nearly smashed into a car on the corner where the gang hung out. Fortunately (or not, depending on how you look at it), the other car was driven by another member of Murder, Inc., Seymour "Blue Jaw" Magoon, who just happened to be the best friend of Buggsy. Buggsy proceeded to get into the car of Magoon (who was given his nickname because of his eternal six o'clock shadow on his face) and drove off.

Such was the evidence that Reles and Dukey gave to the court. Goldstein and Strauss must have realized that they were in a predicament as soon as they heard the evidence given against them. Strauss, who would have known that there would be plenty of other indictments against him for murder, decided to use his wits to get out of this scrape—rather, he'd lose them.

To the astonishment of Goldstein, the handsome, lean Strauss began to act as if he was insane. At the penitentiary where he was held, he refused food, did not shave and hung onto the bars of the cage, screaming like an animal. A picture taken at his trial shows the killer with long hair in the shape of a pompadour and an unkempt beard. Just to show how mad he had become, Pep spent a large part of the trial gnawing on the briefcase of his lawyer. When in the witness stand, he answered questions with non sequiturs: "Did you kill him" would be answered with the unhelpful, "Over easy please, plenty of toast."

These actions may have given the press something to write about but did not impress the court. It impressed the chirpy Buggsy even less. "Gee Pep, you make me sick to look at you!" was the chunky assassin's observation of the degeneration of his colleague.

Buggsy, however, had other things to think about. The knowledge that Reles had turned against him was bad enough. Another witness against him completely shattered the cheerful killer. Blue Jaw Magoon, the friend and bosom buddy of Buggsy, now took the stand. In an effort to save his own skin, the hit man had showed how much honor there is among thieves and gave evidence against his old friend.

If there had been court television at this time, the following incident would have been a showstopper. Buggsy, seeing his body in the chair, stood up and shouted, "Tell the truth Cee! My life depends on you Cee!"

The solid gangster looked at his old comrade, his face going gray. However, he had a job to do, so Magoon went into the box and did something that would guarantee that his friend would be found guilty: he told the truth.

He explained to the court how Buggsy told him that "we've just burned a guy." He told the court how Buggsy had forgotten that there could be prints of the can of gasoline they had used to burn Puggy. He told the court that they had gone to Sheepshead Bay for a meal and that Pep, after ordering his favorite meal of sturgeon, complained that he could still get lockjaw. He related how Reles had argued with Pep as to whether the strangling of Puggy had been sloppy and of how Pep had come back on the Kid.

The defense team must have understood that they were dealing with an impossible task to get the two killers off the hook.

Buggsy's lawyer was unable to present a single witness to help his client. Pep continued with his insanity act, despite the fact that doctors were called to say that the act was just an act. The pleas of the defense lawyers were to no avail. After just ninety-five minutes, the jury, which had been sent out by Judge John J. Fitzgerald, came back with its decision. Walter H. Woodward, the foreman of the jury, read the verdict: "Guilty of murder in the first degree as charged."

If ever fact proved stranger than fiction, it was so now. Strauss, the tall, debonair assassin, realizing that it was time to pay the hangman, stared at the jury without speaking, his long hair now something of a laughing stock among the persons in the court.

Goldstein, however, in an action that owed more to the gallows humor of England in the eighteenth century than to an American courtroom in the twentieth, suddenly said, "Could I say something, don't we deserve a little word?"

"No statement at this time," replied the judge, somewhat taken aback at this lack of judicial propriety.

"We want to thank the jury for what they come up with," said the chirpy gangster, seemingly oblivious to the direction he had received from his elder and better, "with that kind of testimony, you had to come in with what you did." The jury may have been forgiven for being a little astonished at receiving congratulations from a man about to get a mild shock for what he had been doing over the past few years. (These snatches of conversation are from the book *Murder, Inc.* by the prosecuting attorney Burton Turkus, an invaluable source of information for the state of gangdom in the interwar years.)

Only a few days later, the pair of hit men were brought back to the court so that the official sentence could be read out. Buggsy's performance now would go down in the folklore of gangdom. In front of Judge Fitzgerald, Buggsy *officially* had his say.

"I want to first thank the court for the charge he made that is sending us to our death, I only wish it applied to you, judge," he said. The judge remained silent.

"Before I die," continued Buggsy, in this most odd courtroom valediction, "there is one thing I would like to do: I would like to pee up your leg, Judge."

"What's that?"

"I would like to pee up your leg, judge"

"One moment, one moment!" spluttered the indignant legal eagle.

"You cannot go to your death in a nice way," said the irrepressible gangster in a rather bizarre display of logic, "so you might as well go in a bad way."

The court must have tittered at this display of criminal nonchalance. Buggsy subsided, for a while, while the debonair Harry Strauss was described as giving his partner a completely detached glance.

The judge now passed judgment, thinking that the dignity of the law would now be shown. This was some hope, given the way Buggsy had already behaved.

"Having been tried and found guilty of murder in the first degree, the sentence is mandatory upon the court," the judge said as he glared at Buggsy. "The sentence of the court is that you be put to death."

"In the electric chair!" butted in Buggsy, who must have felt it would be just as good to be fried for a piece of wisecracking than a murder.

"In the manner and in the place provided by law, during the week beginning November 4th, 1940," pontificated Judge Fitzgerald, who must now have been wishing he had never been given the case.

"I will take it tomorrow and be satisfied!" exclaimed Buggsy, showing his determination to get the last word.

The following day, the two men were handcuffed and taken to a car that would transport them to Grand Central Station. A mob of newsmen was waiting for them. As usual, Buggsy did all the talking, determined to make a show before being sent to the "Big House up the river."

"I would die happy," he exclaimed, "if I could knock off Turkus and take care of Judge Fitzgerald." More seriously, he spat out, "Just tell that rat Reles I'll be waiting for him. Maybe it will be in hell, I do not know, but I will be waiting, and I bet I got a pitchfork."

This was not the only little performance Mr. Buggsy got to give to the press. Just to give a show, he began to jump up and down and bark like a seal. Harry Strauss, aware that his insane act had fooled nobody, cracked a smile at this.

"I will give you all the pictures you want," remarked Buggsy, "when I come out in a wooden box." After a brief silence, he continued: "Pity I can't hold Reles's hand when I sit in that chair. Reles in one hand and that dirty bastard Magoon in the other."

It appears that Buggsy continued to rattle on all the way up the Hudson River. Strauss only deigned to throw a shoe at reporters who came too close to him.

Only at the gates of the forbidding prison, where so many criminals had ended their lives, did the chunky gangster seem to lose control: "I don't want to go in there, I never killed nobody." It appears that very few people believed him.

On June 12, 1941, the two premier hit men of Murder, Inc. paid the hangman. It appears that Buggsy was very impatient to get the affair over with. In the long, long wait in the execution cell, he remarked to his guards: "What's the use of me sitting here, why don't you put me in the chair and get it over with."

It appears that at the last, the laughing gangster seemed to grasp the extent of his predicament. He refused to see his wife and family, probably not wanting to embarrass them. At 11:03 a.m., with his head shaven and wearing the execution outfit given to condemned criminals, the wisecracking gangster went quickly to the chair and paid the hangman and the American republic for his crimes.

Only a few minutes later, Harold Strauss came out to sit on the same chair. The debonair gangster—who in his heyday had spent an hour at his barber every day, only slept on silken sheets and dressed in sixty-dollar suits—had only seen one person before he paid the hangman: Evelyn Mittleman, the "Kiss of Death Girl." Showing a loyalty that touched some bystanders, she came to see her murderous lover before he made his final exit. Realizing that his insanity act had fooled no one, Pep had had a wash and shave so that his ladylove could see him in his normal, dapper state. (According to his great-nephew, his mother and father did not come to see him; they spent their time listening to the radio, with their daughter, while his son paid his last respects to his girlfriend.)

Shortly before 11:06 a.m., the tall, handsome hood walked out into the execution chamber with a half-sneer on his face, looking, to the witnesses, very, very cool.

He was strapped into the chair. The mask was placed over his head, and his body was wracked with the thousands of volts poured into him.

In the words of one historian, "The syndicate had lost its best hitter."

The runty Happy Maione and the hulking Abbandando should have had an appointment with the executioner before Strauss and Goldstein. A slight error by Judge Taylor meant that in his summing up a reversible error had been made. To the dismay of Turkus and company, the two murderers had gotten a retrial. Once again, Reles was wheeled out to inform on his accomplices; once again he put in a stellar performance. The only thing that stood out in this trial was the fact that the Kid said that they may have gone over to Happy's house to commit a murder.

At this, the runty, nasty little gangster jumped up. "You dirty bastard," shrieked the outraged hood. "In my house! You was never in my house you bastard!"

To show his indignation, Happy seized a glass of water and threw it at Reles. Everyone in the courtroom ducked, except the Kid. Someone observed that Happy threw the missile with his left hand. The man who had hit the unfortunate Rudnick had also been left-handed.

The results were the same: Happy and the Dasher were found guilty again and followed Strauss and Goldstein up the river to the Big House and, on February 19, 1942, followed them into the hot seat.

The bodies of the two men were given to their families for burial. At the burial of the Dasher, his brother Rocco attacked a newsman assigned to cover the funeral.

Somehow, nobody was surprised that it happened.

Chapter 9

THE KID TRIES A SWAN LAKE

The powers that be in the syndicate were, by now, getting very alarmed. With four members of Murder, Inc. now suffering the fates of the chair, it was essential that the Kid be stopped from talking.

The use of a judicious bribe to Reles would obviously be no good at all. Once someone has left the organization, there is no coming back. Both the syndicate and Reles knew this. But how to stop the Kid from talking?

Given the obvious importance of Reles to the authorities, an around-the-clock watch was kept on him. The place where he was held was the Half Moon Hotel, a residence that would soon become a mecca for tourists of a ghoulish bent.

The watch over the Kid did not seem to be a duty that many police officers enjoyed; the Kid, probably because of his situation, became even more obnoxious and vile than usual. He refused to wash and ate like a pig, with the result being that he began to smell like a sewer and ballooned in weight. Getting drunk, he would insult everybody, spit in their faces and generally become obnoxious. Things were not helped at all by the visits of Rose Reles to see her husband.

It can be understood that Mrs. Reles had quite a few things on her mind when visiting her husband: the fact that the man who was the father of her children had been shown to be a coldblooded murderer; the fact that she could only visit him when he was in the presence of police officers; and the obvious physical and moral disintegration of her husband. These were not conditions that are conducive to a happy marriage. The police began to report screaming and shouting when the two met. It became obvious to the Kid that his wife, the woman who had probably managed to get him to go to the police in the first place, wanted a divorce. All of the work, all of the betrayals and all of the heartache (if the Kid could be said to have had a heart) were in vain. On November 11, 1941, on the sixth floor of the Half Moon Hotel, Reles must have gone to sleep a very sad man.

On the morning of the twelfth, an employee from an adjacent building noted a body lying on the roof of the first floor of the Half Moon Hotel. (The second and higher floors were set back from the first floor, so the ceiling of the first floor was also a roof.)

A detective was called and, upon climbing out onto the roof of the first floor, found the body about twenty feet away from the wall, facedown on the roof. Upon turning the body over, the detective saw that it was Reles. The detective looked up to see an open window on the sixth floor. The Kid, as was later confirmed, had "fallen" forty-two feet from the room in which he was guarded. It was concluded that he had landed in a sitting position, which resulted in him breaking his spine at the fourth and fifth vertebrae. The fall had also ruptured his spleen and liver. His body was filled with blood. It was estimated that he had lived for almost half an hour after the fall. It is worth speculating if he did meet Goldstein in the other place and whether Buggsy did indeed have a pitchfork.

The death of the most important stool pigeon in the history of the American republic caused an explosion of rage throughout the higher echelons of the New York police force. Taking into account that Reles was supposed to have been guarded night and day, and that there was always supposed to be a police officer in his room when he slept, the termination of his existence was somewhat odd.

Some other facts that came to light seemed to confuse rather than enlighten those investigating the affair: he was fully clothed and wearing new shoes; he was in possession of only a few dollars; and his room was covered with empty bottles and newspapers. Interestingly, a wire was attached to a radiator in his room, which itself was tied onto some sheets that had been knotted into the shape of a rope. The sheets only reached down to the floor below. So what happened?

The next few weeks were taken up with the study of the death of Reles, who, rather crassly but with brutal accuracy, was nicknamed "the canary who could sing but could not fly." Various theories were articulated as to how this prize specimen met his end. Some said that it was an attempt by Reles to pull a joke on his police guards: he tied a rope to the radiator, let himself out of the window and then had planned to swing into the window of the floor below like a demented Tarzan, run up the stairs and surprise his guards. Taking into account that the sheets would not have been able to support his weight when he let himself out, this theory can be quickly discounted. The idea of him doing a Tarzan act is also a little hard to swallow. Others say that he wanted to commit suicide. This can be discounted by the numerous statements of police officers who said that they had never met a man with a more complete sense of self-worth or self-preservation than Reles.

This leaves only one more suggestion: that he tried to escape, knotting the sheets to aid him in crawling out of the window, dropping down to the first-floor roof and escaping. The plan failed, owing to the fact that the sheet rope snapped, precipitating Reles to the floor and his maker (and to Goldstein, presumably).

This interesting little story seems to ignore the fact that Reles was found more than twenty feet away from the wall. To be found that distance away from the wall seems to show that either Reles took a running jump from the window in order to escape or that he was pushed out of the window for other reasons.

At this point, the reader must understand what Reles had done so far: he had managed to send four men to the chair and had information on literally dozens more. The union and industrial criminal Lepke Buchalter was already facing a murder charge, with Reles as a chief witness. If Buchalter, the most feared of all the syndicate heads, could go to the chair, what next? Reles had got to go and go quick. But how?

The established knowledge on this affair seems to point the finger at the "prime minister of the underworld," Frank Costello, the man whom Masseria so despised for his dealings with politicians. Costello, according to the several sources this author has used, distributed the huge bribe of $50,000 ($100,000 according to others) to the police to save the mob the trouble of dealing with the Kid themselves. It is said that the police whacked the Kid on the head with a nightstick, dressed him and then jointly threw him out of the window. (Another source suggests that the police were bribed to stay away from the room while the mob members themselves did the job.)

Taking into account the rather cozy relationship the police seemed to have with the mob at this time, not to mention political relationships, compliments of Mr. Costello, this seems to be the most obvious solution to the Reles problem. If there are any further doubts on this matter, it should be stressed that the Brooklyn district attorney, William O'Dwyer, later mayor of New York, was subjected to bitter criticism for the way he handled the case of Reles and the men Reles accused of being part of the syndicate. Albert Anastasia and Bugsy Siegel were the next in the firing line regarding the testimony of Reles. When the Kid did his *Swan Lake* dive out of the window on that fateful November day, many people—police officers, gangsters and politicians—would have been more than just a little relieved that the canary had stopped singing.

Chapter 10
LEPKE AND GURRAH

The enforcement arm of the syndicate, Murder, Inc., had been put under the executive arm of Louis Buchalter. Buchalter (or Lepke, a nickname meaning "little Louis") would not have had difficulty in giving orders to this squad of assassins since, according to those who know him best, "Louis loved to hurt people."

Buchalter, born in 1897 to a law-abiding family, had started to go off the rails when his father died and his mother left him (for Colorado) to be brought up by a sister. The rest of Buchalter's family were perfectly respectable: one of his brothers became a dentist and another a pharmacist, while a sister of his became the headmistress of a public school; Louis rapidly moved down into the sewers of crime in New York. By 1915, he had met another thug, Jacob "Gurrah" Shapiro. They specialized in stealing from street vendors, Buchalter being the brains and Shapiro the brawn. Shapiro rapidly got the nickname "Gurrah" from his habit of shouting "Get out of here" in a thick New York accent.

The shopkeepers of the area, terrified and not trusting of the police, thought that they had no choice but to pay up. They thought that they had gotten a break from this pair's machinations when Buchalter was sent to Sing Sing prison for burglary. He came back to the open air a different person.

It appears that he had thought about how he could control the rackets by brain and not brawn. He and Gurrah would appear in a bakery or a clothes factory and point out that it would be in the interests of the employer to cut them in for the profits—if they did not want the business to be burned down or a strike called.

The bitter labor wars of the period helped Buchalter and Gurrah; the unions needed muscle to fight back against the goons the employers used. By offering their services, they could give the unions muscle. They would have to be given positions on the payroll, of course.

Soon Lepke had under his control the dressmakers of the city of New York, the bakeries, leather makers and many of the restaurants. The corrupt head of the Federal Bureau of Investigation (FBI), J. Edgar Hoover (called by this author's father "J. Edgar Garbage"), was telling the truth for once when he called Buchalter "the worst industrial racketeer in America!"

The lifestyle this brought to Buchalter was princely. He regularly wintered in California and Florida, often took himself and his family off to Germany to stay in the most luxurious spas and, like Luciano, was often seen on the racetracks.

Unlike Luciano, Buchalter did not seem to revel in the high life. He was devoted to his wife, whose son he adopted as his own, being, it seems, a doting father. He led a very conservative life—a lifestyle dissimilar to thousands of other Americans only for its opulence. Buchalter seemed to have accomplish the American dream.

But for him, it was death and corruption that would put him on the road to riches. The story of Joe Rosen is an example of this. Rosen worked in the garment industry, which Buchalter, following his usual way of doing business, had managed to infiltrate. He took over Rosen's business and forced Rosen to become an employee in his own company. Buchalter promised to take care of him, and Rosen asked for help when the new employer sacked him.

Buchalter got Rosen a job driving for a trucking firm, where Rosen, who must have been a very odd creature, got fired again. Out of work for several months, Rosen managed to open a candy store, but this went downhill very rapidly. Buchalter got Rosen another driving job, which this worthy soon quit. Buchalter gave Rosen some money and told him to leave the city for a long time.

Rosen, who seems an unlucky individual, lasted a week out of the city before he came back to see his sick wife. He came back to the candy store, and Buchalter heard a rumor that Rosen was threatening to go to Dewey and tell all. Whether this was the truth, or whether Rosen was wanting some more money, is hard to say. When Buchalter heard that Rosen was back in town, according to some observers, he lost his temper for the first time in his life. "That son of a bitch Rosen is shooting his mouth off," the normally placid Buchalter was heard to say. "He's got to go!"

The contract on this strange creature, unsurprisingly, went to Pep Strauss. Compared to the death of Rudnick, this contract would prove to be easy. The usual routine was followed: the gang looked over the area where they would kill the target, and a car was stolen to get the gang to the place of slaughter. A comparative newcomer, Sholem Bernstein, was brought along to steal the car. The restaurateur Louis Capone came along to show Bernstein where to drive the car and where to dump it afterward.

The rest of the operation went like clockwork. Early on a summer's morning in 1936, Pep Strauss and Mendy Weiss were to be found outside of Rosen's candy store. Just after 7.30 a.m., Rosen opened his store, and soon after, Strauss and Weiss walked in. Before he could say a word, the slim Strauss and the hulking Weiss opened fire. Rosen, the sad loser, had come to the end of his life, and it is only to be hoped that he felt no pain.

An autopsy performed later on the unfortunate shopkeeper found that ten bullets had perforated Rosen. All of them were concentrated in an area that could have been covered by a hat. To the bewilderment of the police investigators, six of the bullets were found in the walls of the store, while four were found embedded in the floor. Why on earth would the killer have shot Rosen four times while he was dead on the floor? If he had been lying down, why had the bullets appeared in the wall?

The answer came back some years later, when Reles was doing his canary interpretation to the authorities. The hulking Mendy Weiss had started shooting at Rosen and shot him six times. Rosen was probably dead before he hit the floor. At this point, the kill-crazy Pep Strauss took a hand; to the fury of his fellow hit man, he then shot Rosen four times while the man, now a corpse, lay dead on the floor.

The death of Rosen went unpunished for several years, while Buchalter and his moronic friend Shapiro went on to dominate both the unions and the management of several industries in New York and, in the process, make themselves a fortune. A perfect example of this is the way they managed to dominate the painting trade.

A strike was threatened by the house painters of New York, and the employers promptly hired the help of one "Li'l" Augie Orgen to break it for them. After the obligatory bribe was handed over ($50,000 according to those in the know), Orgen, using the persuasive methods he had at hand, convinced the painters to go back to work. Lepke and Gurrah were part of Orgen's team at this point and, like most ambitious men, were planning on higher things.

A slight glitch arose with this particular dispute when it was decided by the powers that be that the mob should not be involved in this dispute. Orgen was requested to keep out of the strike; also, just to show that the mob understood the principles of the law of the jungle, and in the name of fairness, Orgen was asked to hand the money back to the disgruntled employers.

Well, $50,000 being $50,000, Orgen was a little reluctant to obey this fiat. To the fury of the mob, he flatly refused to follow the order and, as a bodyguard, hired the infamous Jack "Legs" Diamond. Even by the very low standards of the time, Diamond was regarded as a thug. Orgen also should have been far more particular in his choice of thug; Diamond got his nickname according to some observers from the fact that he ran from trouble as soon as he could. He betrayed nearly everyone he ever met until, while asleep in a hideout in Albany in upstate New York, he was betrayed in the same way. A couple of hit men, made aware of his location by a traitor, walked into his room, one taking hold of his ears while the other shot him three times in the head.

When one ignores the dictates of the mob, it is usually a signal for disaster. On October 15, 1927, the inevitable happened. Orgen and Diamond were walking along a street in Manhattan. As in all of the best gangster movies, a black sedan moved toward them. In it were Lepke and Gurrah. One of them leapt out (the various experts on the mob disagree who) and drilled Orgen with four bullets. Diamond, according to some witnesses, jumped away as soon as he saw danger threatening, while Gurrah and Lepke drove off.

A few days later, the two assassins walked into a police station and surrendered themselves to the police, explaining that they understood that the authorities wanted to speak to them over the termination of Orgen. The police, given the nonexistent help of Mr. Diamond, were forced to admit that they had no case at all. Lepke and Gurrah were told that they could go. To ensure that they would not be taken out by Orgen sympathizers, the police gave them an escort of cops to their homes. (It would be bad publicity for a hit man to be taken out next to a police station.) The more perceptive of the police must have been enraged to perform this act, since it would show just what the normal citizens of New York could expect of the American justice system when a pair of thugs was given an escort for having killed a competitor.

The results of this hit were just as inevitable as the refusal of Orgen to cough up the cash: Diamond, when quizzed by the police, told them that he did not know who had shot Orgen; and Lepke and Gurrah took over the organization of Orgen and control of the painters' union and, just to be on the safe side, managed to muscle in on the employers association as well. This way they could rip off both management and unions.

By arranging strikes, murdering honest union reps and throwing articles such as stink bombs and fire bombs into various properties, such as warehouses, garment factories, cinemas and more, Lepke and Gurrah began to be "invited" onto the boards of both unions and management. By the mid-1930s, Lepke and Gurrah had controlling interests in the clothing industry and the bakery industry, as well as control of the cinemas through the motion picture operators union.

One of the reasons for Buchalter's success in his mercantile career was shown in 1933 when Buchalter had one of his rare brushes with the law.

A federal grand jury indicted both Lepke and Gurrah along with 156 others for violating antitrust laws in the fur industry, in which the lethal duo had some interests.

In 1935, the two of them were convicted and sentenced to two years in the slammer and a $10,000 fine. This was merely a slap on the wrist for the labor goons, but the authorities congratulated themselves on, for once, putting someone in the mob behind bars.

Then Judge Martin T. Manton took a hand. Manton was regarded as being one of the most corrupt judges in the history of the American judiciary. He was so well known for his dishonesty that he is the only judge to appear in the Mafia encyclopedia compiled by Carl Sifakis. Manton, who in his not-so-esteemed career would make decisions on an over-the-counter basis (i.e., give him a bribe at court and he would give a decision in your favor) and end up being convicted for corruption, promptly allowed Lepke and Gurrah to leave the slammer and later reversed the convictions.

The mob used Manton many times, paying him royally for his efforts. The famous scene in the film *The Godfather* where Marlon Brando, playing the gangster Vito Corleone, arranges the release of some of his crew from custody with the help of sympathetic judges is very close to the truth. The unholy alliance of the mob, money and the judiciary was one of the main reasons why the mob was able to get started in America.

To the horror of the police and the federal authorities, Lepke and Gurrah walked free to continue their vile careers in several other industries. The "Gold Dust" twins (the nickname given to them owing to their golden touch in their business activities) seemed free to continue for as long as their pockets were long and as long as judges were, if not cheap, bribable.

The lifestyle of Lepke was now becoming increasingly ducal. He took frequent holidays in California and Florida. He visited Hot Springs in Arkansas, which, owing to the efforts of the gangster Owney Madden, was being turned into a sort of rest home for the mob. The stately spas of Carlsbad in Germany were graced with the presence of Lepke on many occasions. In one incident, Lepke came before a court in New York and explained that he had not been able to attend owing to the fact he was on holiday in Europe.

To look at Lepke was to see a man who you would not pick out in a crowd. Unlike Gurrah, whose squat frame, froglike face, hooded eyes and ferocious manner seemed to terrify everyone who met him, Lepke was personally very restrained. Of normal height and a slim build, Lepke had a longish nose and small, rather sad eyes that reminded many people of the face of a sad spaniel. He wore conservative suits and, unlike many of his colleagues (Siegel, Luciano and Al Capone), was not a womanizer. He married Betty Wasserman, the daughter of an English barber, adopted her son and led a life of quiet domestic contentment. Both his wife and her son later stated that Lepke was always the perfect husband and father who was hardly ever known to raise his voice at home.

At the workplace, though, everything was different; if Charles Luciano was nicknamed "Lucky" and Frank Costello the "Prime Minister," Louis was always known as "Judge Louis."

"Lepke loves to hurt people," one shrewd observer noted, which of course is one of the reasons why Lepke was able to continue for so long in business.

Then things began to change.

Chapter 11
THE GREAT LEPKE TREK

The conviction of Luciano sent shock waves throughout the underworld. If the great Charlie Lucky could be convicted, what could happen to the rest of the mob?

Meyer Lansky, the financial mastermind, made a decision that enabled him to remain, more or less, a free man for the rest of his life—by deciding to lead a very low-key life, to avoid any publicity and to keep away from violence if he could possibly avoid it. (When he died in Florida, in a very modest home, the financial mastermind of the mob was worth at least $200,000,000.)

Lepke, as could be expected, decided otherwise.

Realizing that the good old days of the mob were numbered and that he could be next in the firing line, Lepke decided to cover his tracks by simply murdering anybody who he thought could be a threat. People like the sad loser Rosen began to pile up on the streets of New York.

The list of people taken out on the orders of Judge Louis is a long and sad one: Leon Scharf, November 1938; Joseph Miller, a former business partner of Louis, taken out in November 1939; Albert Plug Shulman, April 1939; Irving Penn, mistaken for a rival of Louis, May 1939; and Hyman Yuran, another former business partner of Louis, whose body was discovered in a lime pit—among others.

A survivor of this purge was one Max Rubin, who was another associate of Buchalter who was given the death sentence by the judge. In October 1937, while walking home after giving evidence regarding Buchalter's rackets, Rubin, while leaving an underground station, suddenly found himself falling down on the street. It later emerged that in true Mafia style a friend of Rubin, Paul Berger, had been ordered by Buchalter to point out his friend to a hit man from out of town. Berger had the usual problem of division of loyalties and, of course, decided to obey orders and help his friend be killed.

The hit man duly trailed Rubin, put a bullet through the back of his head and walked away. The shot left Rubin with neck and nerves shattered, with the result that his head was always crooked, but he survived. Buchalter would regret this.

Buchalter could not get Dewey, though. Dewey had been enraged as to the manner in which Judge Manton had released Lepke from prison. Believing that if he got Lepke he would strike a deathblow to the underworld in New York (which just goes to show how little he and anybody else understood the power and extent of the mob), Dewey, eager to get some kudos to help his election to state governor, went after Lepke with all he had.

Lepke began to realize that he was faced with an opponent who could not be killed, bribed, ignored or phased out. Lepke found that his phones were tapped, the offices of the unions he ran were raided and the accounts seized and police followed him everywhere.

To some extent, Lepke was his own worst enemy; besides the usual union and management scams, Lepke had gotten involved in the area that had proved to be the downfall of Lucky Luciano himself: drugs.

Contrary to the suggestion given in the book and the film *The Godfather*, the mob has been into drugs up to its eyeballs. Luciano himself was a dope addict when he was sent to prison. Stepping into his shoes, Lepke proceeded to bribe large numbers of federal customs officials in order to smuggle the profitable powder into America. The result was that Dewey targeted Lepke, in the next few months, on state charges of extortion from the bakery industry and, by the federal government, on the drug problem.

Buchalter was far too shrewd an operator to fail to see that he was now the target of the government's wrath. Coolly calculating his options, he decided to go "on the lam" (a disappearing act).

Buchalter apparently called a meeting of the great and the bad in gangland to tell them the news. Lansky, Siegel, Albert Anastasia, Moey "Dimples" Wolensky and Longy Zwillman (the boss of Newark) were all there, listening with what can be described as some interest to what the famous Judge Louis was going to tell them.

He informed them that he and Gurrah would go underground. Only Albert Anastasia would know where they were in hiding. The rackets he had under his charge would be put in the meaty hands of Mendy Weiss, but he would follow Buchalter's directives.

The members of the board of directors, probably happy to have such a pair of murderous individuals out of their hair, gave their blessings to the enforced separation.

Buchalter went on the lam—and into the folk history of gangdom. When it was realized that the Gold Dust twins were on the run, authorities began to make an unparallel effort to catch them; tens of thousands of wanted posters were put up throughout the length and breadth of the republic. They were sent to schools, police stations and baseball parks; they were hung in railway stations and foreign consulates. And the inevitable sightings were observed.

Buchalter was seen in England, Poland, the Caribbean and in most of the states of America. The "catch Buchalter" craze seemed to take on the entire nation.

The various police and federal organizations began an unprecedented crackdown on organized crime, severely affecting the mob's organization (and, more importantly, its pocketbook). In a very rare display of loyalty, Zwillman was brought before a grand jury and asked if he knew the whereabouts of the location of Judge Louis.

"I've not seen him in three years," came back the mendacious reply, "and I think he is clean morally."

This particular display of honor among thieves cost Zwillman six months in the slammer. The tide slowly began to turn against the ice-cool gang lord, however. His lethal partner, Shapiro, possessing none of the strength of character of his quiet associate, could not take life in the shadows. He began to complain of chest pains and shortness of breath. Realizing that he could not continue on the run, the squat thug surrendered to the authorities in April 1938. As a result of his activities, he was given a life sentence.

Shapiro was given an extra twelve years of life to spend contemplating the fruits of his labor. Apparently he died utterly unrepentant, claiming that if more violence had been used, especially against Dewey, he would have been a free man still.

Buchalter, however, still remained in hiding. He was not in foreign parts, other parts of America or even hiding in Albany, à la Diamond. He remained in Brooklyn all the time, at one time living near a police station.

The months of hiding turned into years, and the mob began to be hit harder and harder by the crackdown. Then, in August 1939, Buchalter surrendered to none other than J. Edgar Hoover himself.

What on earth had made this ice-cool king of the unions and employers associations surrender? There are a number of stories that have turned up over the years; some say that J. Edgar Hoover had been put under so much pressure that he gave a flat demand to the mob: "Buchalter or else!"

Another story, which seems to be much nearer the truth, is that the members of the mob were getting more and more exasperated by the amount of pressure being put on them. If the pressure continued, their incomes would have been affected. If Buchalter were in police custody, then the heat would probably be turned off and conditions would return to normal—there would also be the fact that someone would have to take over the rackets of Judge Louis. Ahh.

Luciano, now in a federal slammer but still consulted regarding the mob's problems, fully understood the problem and readily gave his permission for the judge to be betrayed by his own cohorts. How could this cunning man be tricked into surrendering?

Luciano decided that Buchalter would have to be conned into surrendering, the same way he had managed to con Masseria into accepting a date that would lead to his termination in the Nuova Villa restaurant—Maranzano had been knifed in his own office.

Buchalter, after almost two years of hiding, was, even for a man of his own strong character, beginning to feel the pressure. When one of his most trusted associates, "Dimples" Wolensky, approached him with some news regarding a deal about a possible sentence, Buchalter was very interested.

According to Wolensky, a deal had been made with Hoover himself regarding the fate of Buchalter: he would be given five years if he surrendered to Hoover himself, and no other charges would be brought against him, state or federal.

Buchalter checked his options. If he did not accept the deal, he would be on the run for many years, and who knows what would happen to him? If he took it, he might be betrayed, but his own friend, Wolensky, told him that it was a certain thing.

The only fly in the ointment was the attitude of Anastasia. With brutal logic, the Mad Hatter stated, "If they can't get you, they can't harm you; once they have their hands on you, not all the deals in the world can save you."

Louis "Lepke" Buchalter, *center*, handcuffed to J. Edgar Hoover. *Courtesy of the* New York World-Telegram *and the Sun Newspaper Photograph Collection, Library of Congress.*

Buchalter, who, like many in his position, now just wanted to believe what he had heard, decided to surrender.

On August 24, 1939, in one of the most grotesque arrests in the history of the American republic, Anastasia was driving Buchalter in a car. To give him some cover, the sister-in-law of Louis Capone was in the back of the car holding a baby, which, incidentally, she had borrowed from a neighbor. (This would be the second time the Mad Hatter would use a baby for cover. There are some interesting psychological conclusions to be drawn here!)

Buchalter got into the car, which was driven a few blocks to where another car waited, in which was waiting the gossip columnist Walter Winchell. Buchalter got out of the car and went over to Winchell's vehicle, where J. Edgar Hoover, for once doing something for the benefit of America, joined him.

Almost as soon as he was in the car, Buchalter realized that he had been told a fairy tale: there was no deal. This was shown when Buchalter was turned over to the federal government, which sent him away for fourteen years on a narcotics charge.

The feds then turned him over to Dewey, who promptly hammered him with thirty years to life for his bakery scams. To rub ointment into the wound, it was announced that the two sentences would be consecutive, so the judge was looking at about fifty years in the slammer.

Then things began to get really bad for the judge.

The Servants Follow Their Boss

In 1941, with Buchalter now having time to meditate on the state of honor among his thieves, the bombshell broke: he was to be put on trial with the suave Louis Capone and Buchalter's personal aide, the hulking Emanuel Weiss, for the murder of Rosen. The story behind this trial was, of course, the decision of the Kid to rat on his friends. After he had sent Pep Strauss, Happy Maione, the Dasher Abbandando and Buggsy to the chair, the Kid then lined up to take out Judge Louis. He gave his story regarding Buchalter concerning the Rudnick murder before a grand jury and then decided to try to emulate the feat of Daedalus from the Half

Lepke Buchalter, under armed guard, attending a court hearing. He would later be the richest man in America to go to the chair.

Moon Hotel. The statement he had made, however, could be used in evidence against Buchalter. As a result of the confessions of Reles, other members of the syndicate began to talk—the most noticeable was Albert "Tick-Tock" Tannenbaum. The son of the archetypal nice Jewish family, Tannenbaum had been given the strange appellation as a result of his nonstop talking while excited.

Tannenbaum and other members of Buchalter's gang proceeded to give evidence against him and his two confederates when it came to trial on November 1941. The mob unrolled its bankroll for this trial of trials and bought the best legal talent available. This was shown by the fact it took twenty-two days for half of the jury to be selected and twelve weeks before the whole of the jury was picked.

Perhaps at this time, Buchalter may have remembered the message that Shapiro had sent to him regarding the decision taken not to hit Dewey: "Told you so!" was the brutal and logical statement from his old colleague.

A battery of witnesses was brought against the three desperadoes; among them was the former friend of Buchalter, Rubin. As he was still probably in pain from the bullet sent into his head on the orders of Buchalter, it can be understood that he was somewhat aggrieved over his old friend.

Rubin told the whole story of the sad life of Rosen: how he was driven out of business by Buchalter, how he was forced to leave the city, how he came back and begged for help, how he was left on his own for months, how he started a candy store and how, toward the end, he died in a pool of his own blood, compliments of Mendy Weiss and Pep Strauss.

Buchalter ordered Rubin out of the city after this murder. Rubin obeyed but soon missed his family. He came back and was told that Buchalter wanted to see him. In true gangster fashion, the meeting took place near Rubin's house in a thunderstorm.

"Max," Buchalter said in his soft voice, "you came back without permission."

"I had to see my wife, Louis."

"Max, you came back without permission."

"Nobody knows I'm in town, Louis."

"How old are you, Max?" said Buchalter in a strange non sequitur.

"Forty-eight."

"That's a ripe age, Max," said Buchalter, as he disappeared into the rain.

It was through conversations such as these, as well as the fact that Rubin now looked on Buchalter with something akin to hatred, that meant that he now had the courage to face the tsar of the industrial shakedown. He mentioned the incident when Buchalter had completely lost it regarding the defiance (if it can be called that) of Rosen. (Tannenbaum, too, was a witness to this incident.)

At one point, the rage and despair of Rubin spilled out into the court; when accused of being an actor and a complete fake, he exploded at the defense counsel: "I was never a murderer, I never did anything wrong till I met Buchalter!"

If this was not an event that would today look good on prime time TV, when "Tick-Tock" Tannenbaum took the stand, he came up with some revelations that had the court gasping.

Albert dropped in on Buchalter just after the Rosen killing. He was sitting in his office when the meaty Mendy Weiss entered, obviously in a bad mood. According to Albert, the following was the gist of the conversation:

Buchalter: "Was everything all right?"

Weiss: "Everything is okay, only that son of a bitch Pep, I gave him orders not to do any shooting, but after Rosen is lying on the floor, Pep shoots him!"

Buchalter: "Okay, as long as everything is clean, what is the difference?"

If Rubin's evidence had taken care of Buchalter, then Tannenbaum's evidence had taken care of Weiss.

Capone's turn came when yet another hit man turned confessor went into the witness box. Seymour "Blue Jaw" Magoon had already sent his friend Buggsy Goldstein to the chair, and now he was going to do the same to Louis Capone.

He mentioned that Capone had been involved in the "Rosen" thing and had mentioned that he had been in a few other hits before. This came as a complete shock to the attorney representing Capone, who, it appears, did not remember the conversation. Magoon's statement was good enough for the jury.

The trial ended on Saturday, November 30. After only four hours of discussion, the jury came back with the verdicts: guilty on all counts for all three witnesses. Buchalter's wife screamed when she heard the verdict.

The three men were told to approach the bench. Buchalter's face showed no emotion whatsoever, but he held on tight to the rail in front of the bench until his knuckles were white; Capone listened defiantly, his jaw thrust out; and Weiss, his gargoyle leer gone, folded his arms while the judge read the sentence that would send them to the chair in Sing Sing:

> *For the murder of Joseph Rosen, whereof he is convicted, is hereby sentenced to the punishment of death. Within ten days the Sheriff of Kings County shall deliver the said prisoners to the Warden of Sing Sing prison, where they shall be kept in solitary confinement, until the week beginning Sunday, January 24th, and in some day on the week appointed, the warden of Sing Sing prison will do execution upon him, in the mode and manner prescribed by the law.*

Louis Capone (left) and Mendy Weiss on their way to Sing Sing. They both look very relaxed about this.

Burton Turkus, the man appointed by Dewey to head the prosecution team, and who had been given the nickname "Mr. Arsenic," was thirty-eight that day. It was a birthday present he would be proud of.

The three men were duly sent up the river to Sing Sing. Anyone who is of a macabre temperament can note in the picture above Louis Capone and Weiss on the train taking them to the hot seat. Capone is smiling at the camera, having most likely made peace with himself; Weiss, at his side, is dressed in the gangster costume of overcoat and trilby and smirks into the camera.

A barrage of appeals was sent off to the relevant courts, which proceeded to examine the facts of the matter for almost eighteen months. It was not until March 1944 that the sentence was officially confirmed by the circuit court of appeals.

On March 2, 1944, the three men—the hulking Weiss, who would play the part of the gangster to the end; the cold-hearted Buchalter; and the suave Capone—were finally prepared for death. Their heads were shaved, and they were clothed in white socks, black trousers, black shirts and white shirts. The three of them were taken to adjacent cells, where, though they could not see, they could speak to one another. With true gallows humor, it was nicknamed "the dance hall."

The condemned men were offered their obligatory last meal. Buchalter chose for lunch steak, salad, chips and pie and for dinner roast chicken, shoestring potatoes and salad. Capone and Weiss said that they would have what their boss would have. In an unforgettable phrase from his book *Tough Jews*, Rich Cohen remarked, "These men would stick to the end, leading him to the unknown, like the servants of the Pharaoh."

While in the dance hall, the three of them found out they had been given another two days of life while Dewey, a good lawyer, studied the case in detail.

"At least we get more good eats!" said the nerveless Weiss to his fellows.

A lot of ink has been spilled over the fact that Buchalter could have pulled a Reles and betrayed his fellow thugs. This is pure fiction. Buchalter was the most powerful man ever to be sent to the chair, and if a deal was made with him—unlike Reles, who was small time—an uproar would have ensued. It would have been like doing a deal with Saddam Hussein—under condition he would survive, while the rest of his household was executed.

The inevitable happened on the night of March 4, 1944. The three men were sent to their creators compliments of the State of New York and the more than two thousand volts pumped into them through the electric chair.

At 11:02 p.m., Capone went first. He had a weak heart, and he could not die on the authorities just after they had gone to all the trouble to execute him. He said not a word while he was strapped in and had the life pulled out of him.

Capone's body was being wheeled out when Mendy Weiss came in. In best gangland tradition, he was chewing a wad of gum. Seated in the chair, he asked permission to speak. It was granted.

"All I want to say is I am innocent and I'm here on a framed up charge. Give my love to my family and everything."

The switch was pulled, and the meaty gangster went to his gods with a lie on his lips.

Buchalter came out last. He stared at the thirty-six newsmen and other witnesses who filled four rows of benches off to one side of the chair. His brisk and defiant step took him to the chair, on which, according to the witnesses, he practically threw himself. His eyes swept over the audience, and unlike Weiss, he made no speech as the lever was pulled and the voltage sent his 165-pound body slamming against the chair.

The man who had robbed his fellow Americans, terrorized them and made a mockery of the American dream at least had the satisfaction of being the richest man in history to fry in the chair.

The tsar of the industrial racketeers was the last of the great Mafia capos to die—officially, at least, which in this context means according to the legal process of the American republic.

He was by no means the only one to go to his gods in a violent manner.

Chapter 12
GENOVESE

THE LAST GODFATHER?

Vito Genovese had pulled himself up the hard way. Born in Italy in 1897, he had immigrated to America and gravitated to crime—unlike the many millions of Italian immigrants who made such a huge contribution to the development of their adopted country. By the 1920s, he had risen to the rank of triggerman for Lucky Luciano, taking out many of this criminal mastermind's enemies. As a result of the Castellammarese War, Genovese became a member of the Luciano crime family, one of the five crime families formed by Luciano and Salvatore Maranzano in 1931 to control and administer the criminal gangs of New York.

Genovese, through a mixture of stealth, cunning and ruthlessness, soon became a top member of the Luciano crew, and his prospects seemed to be getting brighter by the minute as a result of Luciano being sent to the federal slammer in 1936 for a bewildering variety of charges concerning his organization of the prostitution trade in New York. As Genovese was the underboss of Luciano, with his boss now absent Genovese found himself at the head of the largest criminal family in New York, though his tenure of this position would prove to be a distressingly short one.

Luciano had been sent to the slammer owing chiefly to the efforts of the federal prosecutor Thomas Dewey. After Luciano was sent away, Genovese was the next in line for Dewey's attentions.

Dewey must have felt himself spoiled for choice regarding Genovese, who had more skeletons rattling in his cupboard than Dracula. Besides killing the first husband of the beautiful Anna Vernotico—a woman with whom he had fallen madly in love and whom he had married only twelve days after her husband's body, with legs and arms bound, was found strangled—he was also implicated in the death of Ferdinand "the Shadow" Boccia, a gangster with whom he had fallen out after ripping off a businessman in a scam worth $160,000. The fact that Boccia held up a store owned by Tony Bender, a close friend of Genovese, did not help him very much at all.

Genovese, feeling that discretion was the better part of valor, departed to Italy in 1937, taking with him, according to the jaundiced and somewhat unreliable testimony of Anna, $750,000 in cash in a suitcase.

The arrival in Italy of this high-ranking member of the Mafia could, in some eyes, have been rather foolish, since Mussolini, the Italian dictator, had savagely cracked down on the Mafia during his rather inefficient tenure as the new duce.

Genovese, showing the cunning perception needed by any leader in such an organization, managed to cozy up to the Italian leader. The fact that he supplied drugs to Count Ciano, the Italian foreign minister (and the dictator's son-in-law), may have had something to do with this.

Genovese also showed how useful he could be in a more practical matter. In his youth, Mussolini had met a man named Carlo Tesca at a time when both of them shared leftist sympathies (which Mussolini lost after a very short time). Following his rise to power, Mussolini became very agitated over the antics of his old friend, who did not lose his political beliefs quite so easily. Tesca was duly exiled to America, where he proceeded to publish a magazine, *Il Martello*, which gave quite a lot of space to denouncing the brutalities of the regime in Italy.

The Italian dictator raged at this piece of impertinence, and Genovese, seeing an opportunity to ingratiate himself even closer, arranged to have Tesca silenced by means other than a writ for libel. Tesca was duly whacked out on January 11, 1943. The presumed hit man was the then low-ranking Carmine "the Cigar" Galante, soon to prove himself one of the most ferocious killers of the syndicate. Genovese stayed close by the dictator's side until the end of the war, when Mussolini and his mistress were executed and strung up before an appreciative crowd in Lombardy.

Genovese, with typical cunning, promptly offered his services to the new American regime and became a sort of factotum in chief, arranging

Carmine Galante met his maker in a mom and pop store.

everything from running the black market (and, just for show, giving evidence against other criminals in the business) to pimping. Genovese was making millions from these scams when, to his great surprise, he came against an honest man: Orange Dickey, a sergeant in the army's criminal investigation division. Dickey arrested Genovese for widespread smuggling and then was told, through an informant, that he had arrested a man wanted back stateside for murder.

Dickey duly advised the FBI of his capture. Dickey must have felt that there was something odd about his charge, as he later said when visiting Genovese's home that he had never seen a house of such luxury or such an opulent wardrobe for one man. Dickey was about to be taught a lesson in the power that the mob has. For months, no communication was forthcoming about how Genovese should be dealt with. The army ordered him to drop the investigation, as did William O'Dwyer, a former prosecution attorney in Brooklyn. Dickey refused to do so and managed to get Genovese on a ship back to America, ignoring the bribes Genovese offered and, later, the threats against his family.

Vito Genovese. *Courtesy of the* New York World-Telegram *and the Sun Newspaper Photograph Collection, Library of Congress.*

Genovese duly returned to the States. To the astonishment of Dickey, Genovese suddenly became very friendly and relaxed. "Kid," Genovese said to Dickey, "you are doing me a great favor; you are taking me home."

Genovese returned home in January 1948, after an absence of more than seven years, to be promptly arrested for murder. The authorities had two witnesses against Genovese, one of whom, upon hearing of his return from Italy, begged to be put in protective custody. He was put in a police cell and died there, after his food had been poisoned. Genovese went free, and Dickey, in the words of Carl Sifakis, the Mafia chronicler, was left like the ancient mariner in the poem by Coleridge, "a sadder but wiser man."

As more than one authority has pointed out, Genovese would probably not have returned to America on his own; he was earning far too much in Italy to want to. Not only Dickey but also many members of the mob would be distressed at the release of Don Vito.

Chapter 13
COSTELLO AND GENOVESE
THE FIRST CHECK

W ith Genovese breathing down his neck, Costello had to find a way to get some extra protection from Don Vito. In a move of genius, Costello looked to the neighboring state of New Jersey, where his old friend, Willy Moretti, had his fiefdom.

A childhood friend of Costello (he had been best man at Moretti's wedding), Moretti at this time controlled a group of about sixty enforcers in the state, most of his income coming from owning or shaking down casinos. With Moretti at his elbow, Costello could breathe a little more freely.

This feeling of relief was not to last, however; Moretti, an inveterate skirt chaser, proceeded to become infected with a disease that needs no explanation. Always outgoing and something of a motor mouth, Moretti proceeded to act in a way that dismayed Costello and angered the syndicate. He started to bet on horses in races that had not taken place, babble on about mob affairs in public and generally behave in such a way that even capos loyal to Costello started to protest.

Moretti was sent to the West Coast on an enforced holiday by the harassed Costello, only coming back when he became slightly less voluble. This period of enforced silence was not to last long, however, since there would soon occur an episode that would have no short-term effects but would still wake America up to the power of the mob: the Kefauver hearing.

The Settling of Accounts

The release of Genovese in 1946 meant that he could now become the head of the Luciano crime family. Rather confusingly, this family once headed by Lucky Luciano had been led—once Luciano was imprisoned and then exiled—by Genovese and then, following his precipitate departure to Italy, by Frank Costello and then by Genovese again upon his return.

In Genovese's absence, Costello, the master political fixer of the underworld, had allowed his capos a lot of freedom of action. This freedom, together with the political fixes that Costello was able to arrange, meant that many of his capos and triggermen became very rich. It was estimated, by an admittedly very dubious source, that more than forty of the Genovese gang by the end of the 1950s were millionaires. This easygoing state of affairs was ended with the return of Genovese. A reception was held for him at a hotel bearing the most inappropriate title of the Diplomat Hotel. Here Costello, with feelings that can only be imagined, had to escort Genovese to the top of the table.

It appears that Genovese had set himself three targets when he arrived in America: to make the business richer than ever (this goes without saying, since the main business of the mob is to make money); to strengthen his position at the head of the Genovese family; and to become the boss of all bosses.

The extremely immodest ambitions had to be put on the back burner for a while, as some private and extremely embarrassing business had to be settled first.

While he had been away in Italy, Genovese had carefully arranged to have his wife, Anna, looked after by a friend of his, Steve Franse. It was Franse's role to escort Anna to various functions, make sure that she was comfortable and ensure that she did not stray from the path of wifely faithfulness.

In the last aspect, Franse was noticeably lax, as Anna took a number of lovers from both sexes. Franse himself, it appears, warmed himself in the boss's bed.

Anna was not altogether happy about her husband's return. This was not only due to the fact that she could no longer play the free spirit but also to the fact that Don Vito behaved in a manner that a distressingly large number of Mafia wives have had to take for granted. Apart from being a serial philanderer, Genovese had the vulgarity to flaunt his mistresses and girlfriends in front of Anna, a fact that many Mafiosi look on as being uncouth. When she complained, Vito responded in time-honored fashion and promptly belted her, sometimes in public—something that was regarded as being even more uncouth.

Anna was so outraged by this behavior that she took the very unusual step of filing for divorce. Vito promptly threatened to kill her, and when she still refused to buckle, Genovese went for advice from, of all people, Frank Costello, who diplomatically advised him to get a good lawyer. Vito's refusal to kill his wife, it appears, made him lose face in some circles of the mob.

The revelations about the lifestyle of Genovese caused hysterics among the press and the mob. Genovese, according to Anna, possessed a $75,000 house, with improvements worth $100,000; furniture and statues and other antiques worth $250,000; and an astonishing number of $250 suits.

"Vito earned about $40,000 a week," said the courageous wife. "I should know, I kept the books!"

Despite this huge income, Anna, probably wisely, only claimed $350 a week. The judge, who must have been something of a skinflint, gave Anna $300, plus the counsel fees she demanded. The divorce went through, and Anna and Don Vito departed.

Genovese must have felt genuine regard for Anna, since according to the Mafia superinformant Joe Vallachi—whose evidence is not regarded as being very reliable—whenever Genovese later talked of Anna he would begin to cry.

The revelations in court, and the knowledge that Anna had warmed her body with bodies that did not belong to her husband, made Genovese look foolish to his peers, and looking foolish is one thing a Mafia don cannot abide.

Franse was the man Don Vito had left in charge of his wife. He had failed to control her to a marked degree; it was even rumored that he and Anna were planning to live together.

Franse had to be dealt with, and dealt with he was. In June 1953, Franse was invited to the Lido Restaurant in the Bronx. He was there taken out "buckwheats" (meaning that his departure from this world was made as painful as possible). He was savagely beaten up and garroted. His body was dumped in his own car, which was found the next day. Genovese had followed the old Mafia adage to "always kill a brother for revenge"—or, in this case, a lover. Genovese had made sure that Anna would not enjoy a life in which she could share her love with a man she truly adored, and Genovese's honor was secured.

This little domestic spat taken care of, Genovese decided that in order to make the family richer than ever, they should walk up an avenue that was comparatively unexplored: drugs.

In a famous scene from the film *The Godfather*, the Corleone family gather to discuss whether they should start dealing in drugs. The decision taken by the top capo is that no, they should not, as there were too many risks involved.

This was a decision mirrored by the stance Costello took, that it was too risky. The decision on drugs was regarded as being so important that it took a full-scale meeting of the gang bosses, gathering in Cuba, to decide the destiny of their financial actions.

Lucky Luciano, who had quite illegally quit Italy to see how things were going in the old country, chaired the meeting. The drug issue was discussed, and like nearly all summit meetings with the top bananas present, the result was a very unsatisfactory compromise: it would be up to the individual bosses to see what happened in their territory. It appears that not only were Luciano and Costello against the drug traffic but also the urbane Tommy "Three Finger" Lucchese, one of the more civilized chiefs. If the green light had not been given, at least there was no red one, and Genovese cheerfully went ahead with his drug trafficking.

Middle-age Crisis: Costello and Society

It was observed that immediately after the conference at Havana Costello did not appear to be his urbane self; taking into account that he had to accommodate Genovese, this can hardly be regarded as surprising. He took a course that would be taken by the fictional hero Tony Soprano in the TV series of the eponymous name: he went to see a psychiatrist.

The psychiatrist was most unlike the character played by Lorraine Bracco, since the advice given by this worthy, Dr. Richard H. Hoffman, proceeded to mess up the life of his patient even more.

Hoffman's advice to Costello was to mix "with a better class of person." This Costello duly did, hosting a dinner for the Salvation Army at a nifty $100 per plate. It shows the extent of Costello's power that no fewer than four judges of various ranks sat down with the "prime minister of the underworld." Costello must have found their company far more congenial than that of Genovese, whom he had to invite.

The advice given by Hoffman did not appear to work; the papers soon got a hold of the story, and the politicians and judges who attended swore with all the sincerity of the sanctimonious that they did not know the identity of the host. This was regarded as being a little strange by some of the more cynical observers, as each of the guests had received a personal note of thanks from Mr. Costello.

This appears to have taught Costello a lesson, and he never again tried to mix with a better sort of people. This belief was soon compounded when Dr. Hoffman was questioned by the press—he cheerfully gave an account of the visits of the mob lord, in complete violation of patient-doctor confidentiality.

The Mob: TV Entertainment

It seems to be a complete mystery to many people in the twenty-first century as to why the antics of the mob seemed to have been ignored by contemporary Americans. Given the fact that most people in this country had not heard of the syndicate until they saw the *The Godfather*, this can be quite understood. How on earth were the masses of the American people to know of this criminal conspiracy when so few of them came into contact with them and when the sole forms of communication were those of the papers (which did not seem to have the knowledge of the mob that they have now) and the cinema (whose owners would not have been especially favorable to showing films as to how they were being ripped off)?

Frank Costello testifying before the Kefauver Committee investigating organized crime. *Courtesy of the* New York World-Telegram *and the Sun Newspaper Photograph Collection, Library of Congress.*

Another reason is the behavior of the so-called top cop in America, the head of the FBI, the megalomaniacal J. Edgar Hoover. In his long and dishonorable stint at the head of this elite organization, Hoover spent most of his time looking for Communists (who usually were nowhere to be seen); basking in the fact that his men managed to kill John Dillinger, the bank robber; and ordering his agents to catch car thieves (so that the arrest statistics would look good when begging for funds from Congress). He also, as the author Carl Sifakis pointed out, was responsible for one of the greatest con jobs played on the American public: he gave the impression that he was working practically twenty-four hours a day on the job, taking hardly any holidays.

Hoover, in fact, took many holidays, quite often to the racetracks, where he was an enthusiastic, some say degenerate, gambler. Needless to say, the syndicate had a great deal of interest in fixing such races, and when Costello found out Mr. Hoover's foible, Uncle Frank, needless to say, was very interested. He began to pass on tips to the top cop at a furious rate, suggestions that made Hoover a very happy man. So appreciative was Hoover of the efforts of Costello that he once invited him to the Stork Club and told him to "just stay out of my bailiwick."

Costello, who had no interest in Communism or stealing cars, obliged, and for most of his long and unsavory life, Hoover let the syndicate have a clear run for its money. This amiable partnership was smashed, or at the very least shaken, in 1950 with the famous Kefauver hearings.

Estes Kefauver was a federal politician and the chairman of the Senate's committee on interstate commerce. Some thoughtful individuals had been aware of the growing threat of the mob and, in the best American way, delegated one of the Senate's numerous committees to investigate it. Committees had come and gone before; what made this one so special was that the proceedings were televised. Most people did not own television sets, but obliging retailers put them in the windows of their shops for the entranced public to see large-scale crime put on trial for the first time.

A number of leading bosses were called to give evidence. Or at least they were called; little actual evidence was given, since nearly all of them took the Fifth Amendment, which allowed a person to remain silent so as not to incriminate himself.

"Taking the Fifth" became part of the American vernacular and was used, among others, by Jake Guzik of the Chicago mob, who boldly appeared without a lawyer and took the Fifth on the grounds that "he did not want to be discriminated against," and Frank Ericson, a gambler who did not want it to "criminate him."

Also called were Joe Adonis, the handsome Broadway capo, who in the famous words of the historian William Manchester "left the hearings just another overdressed hood." Forced to plead guilty to violating gambling laws, Adonis was given two years in the slammer and was later forced into exile in the sunnier climes of Italy.

Considerable interest was shown when Virginia Hill, who had been the lover of, it seems, most of the mob leadership, was called to the stand. Covered with furs and flashing with diamonds, Ms. Hill, with commendable speed, informed the committee that she had never heard of the Mafia and that some men just happened to give her lots of money. When asked why so many men gave her such a lot of money, her reply—very much sanitized—was: "I am the best godamned lay in the business!"

The feisty Ms. Hill walked out of the room and swore at the astonished journalists, one of whom, Marjorie Farnworth, of the *New York Journal*, was clobbered by a right hook.

Costello was also called to give evidence. What happened next went down in the history of crime TV folklore. Costello's lawyer objected to the fact that his client's face would be shown on the TV. It was agreed that the camera would only film the hands of Uncle Frank. What the committee and the public got was the famous "Hand Ballet." His perfectly manicured hands were seen to fold and crush a handkerchief, to lock and interlock and to pour water into a tumbler, while the committee grilled him about his life and deeds.

Why had he used the name "Saverio" while at an earlier trial? What about the $15,000 that he had received from a local gambler? Did he worry that his telephone was tapped? When he answered in the negative, an employee of a telephone company stated that Costello had called him at regular intervals to check his lines. Costello was duly charged with perjury.

Costello walked out of the hearings to be brought back the following day and questioned about the thing he most feared: his relationship with Bill O'Dwyer, the American brigadier who had been of no help at all to Sergeant Dickey. O'Dwyer had been the Brooklyn district attorney in the early years of Word War II, when his efforts to curb crime in his bailiwick had been seen to be noticeably mild. The fact that this was the time when the famous mob informer Abe Reles had met his end by being thrown through a window from a hotel did not redound to his credit. Both Costello and O'Dwyer were questioned about their respective relationships, and O'Dwyer innocently suggested that he had met Costello in order for him to deal with some troubles with an airfield. The administration of President Harry Truman was so embarrassed at the exposure of O'Dwyer that he was appointed ambassador to Mexico.

Costello was shattered by the hearings and drew an eighteen-month sentence for contempt. His main muscle, Willie Moretti, followed him on to the stand, did not take the Fifth Amendment and proceeded to delight both the public and the committee with his candor.

Committee: "Are you a member of the Mafia?"

Moretti: "No, I do not have a union card!"

Committee: "Are you a member of the mob?"

Moretti: "They call anybody a mob who makes 6 percent or more on anything."

Committee: "Do you know any gangsters?"

Moretti: "Well-charactered people do not need introductions!"

Moretti left the stand, the senators seemingly very pleased at the testimony. "Rather refreshing," was the comment of one of them.

"Thank you very much," said the incorrigible joker of the mob. "You are all invited to my house in Deal when you are down on the shore."

The mob bosses seemed to be very pleased with the antics of Moretti; however, as Costello had feared, the syphilis that Moretti had contracted during his numerous visits to prostitutes was now shattering his brain.

By late 1951, Moretti was babbling about holding a press conference to review gambling in New Jersey. The mob bosses looked on with a mixture of wrath and apprehension at the wreck the once mighty mobster was becoming.

Genovese had the answer.

Don Vito and Costello: Round Two

Genovese had been perfectly aware of the reasons for the friendship with Moretti and Costello: Costello supplied the brain and political and legal contacts, Moretti the brawn and Don Vito was checked—but not mated.

Don Vito realized that if Moretti went Costello's muscle went, too. Not only would Costello be helpless, but the rackets Moretti owned in New Jersey were also going to be up for grabs. Genovese, cunning street fighter that he was, began to lobby for the execution of the motor-mouthed boss.

Not even Costello could save his chum when the safety of all was at stake. Even the staunch Costello ally Anastasia said that the hit had to occur. It would be a "mercy killing," said the murderous gangster, in an unusually tender phrase.

On October 4, 1951, Anastasia telephoned Moretti, complaining of back pains. The generous mobster obligingly drove Anastasia to St. Mary's hospital in New Jersey. Anastasia stayed there all afternoon and was obligingly given both a cure and an alibi.

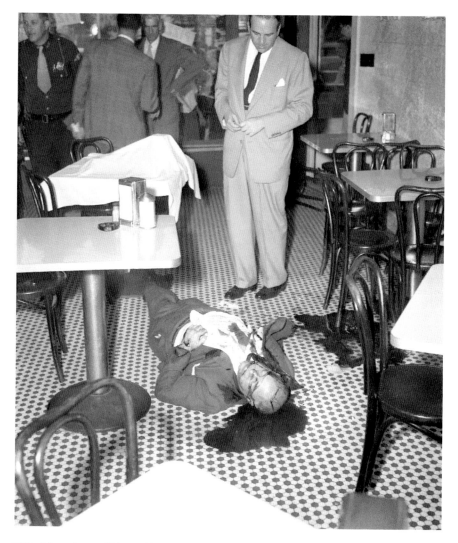

Willy Moretti scored his card in a New York café.

At about 11:30 a.m., Moretti went to a restaurant bizarrely named Joe's Elbow Room. He talked to a group of men (three or four is the number given) in an amiable manner in Italian. The waitress in the café went into the kitchen, and a number of gunshots were heard. When the waitress returned, Moretti was found to be dead on the floor, his left hand on his chest.

In mob lore, the killing had been a "respectful" one: the boss had been allowed to see his killers. Others of a more cynical cast would regard this as absolute rubbish; the reason why Moretti was shot from the front was so that the killers could make no mistake as to whom they had shot.

As Carl Sifakis, the Mafia historian, said, "This could have been a sign of genuine respect, since, after all, everybody liked Willy, they just happened to like him better dead!"

With Moretti dead, Genovese thought that he now had Costello over a barrel and could extend his interests at the expense of the exiled Luciano, Lansky and Costello.

The death of Moretti, however, did not stop Uncle Frank from looking around for more muscle. In an act of diplomatic genius, he hit on the idea of getting another protector—one who would have an entire crime family behind him, one who was too thick to try to take over Costello's influence, one who could be depended on to keep his mouth shut and one who was (hopefully) not infected with VD.

In an inspired choice, Costello picked the "Lord High Executioner," the "Mad Hatter" Anastasia to protect him. The consensus among nearly all historians of the mob is that Costello suggested to the thick-skinned Anastasia that he was a perfectly good crime boss and that he should be the head of the Mangano family, for whom he had been a not-very-loyal underboss for nearly twenty years.

Anastasia's association with the Mangano brothers, Vincent and Phil, was one not burdened with too much friendship. Vincent Mangano was outraged that Anastasia seemed to show more loyalty to Luciano and Costello than to him. The relationship between the arrogant Mangano and his homicidal underboss became so bad that on many occasions the two of them had to be stopped from exchanging blows with each other by their fellow gangsters.

Anastasia was probably trying to get control of the family anyway by the time of the Kefauver hearings, but the suggestions of Costello most likely swung Anastasia in favor of direct action.

On April 18, 1951, Phil Mangano was about to enter a bet on a horse race, when two men approached him and said something that made him enter their car in a hurry.

The following morning, on Brooklyn's Bergen Beach, his body, with three bullets in his brain, was discovered, but without, for some reason, his trousers. This rather odd whacking generated a great deal of interest, so much so that Joe Adonis was asked about this during the hearing of the Kefauver Committee.

Committee: "Who killed Phil Mangano?"

Adonis: "This could not have been a gangland murder; his pants were off when they found him, it was probably a crime of passion!"

This was the last the committee heard of Phil Mangano.

If discovering the reasons for the death of Phil Mangano proved to be difficult, the committee members were on even worse ground when they checked the whereabouts of Vince Mangano, since he was nowhere to be seen—a state of affairs that has persisted to this day.

The commission, the mob's governing body, held an inquiry into the disappearance of Vince Mangano (Phil was not considered to be of any importance). Anastasia accused Vince Mangano of trying to kill him. This theory was backed up to the hilt by Costello. The commission, to the fury of Genovese, accepted this explanation, and Anastasia became the head of one of the five family gangs of New York.

Costello had gotten some more muscle. Unfortunately, he did not get the brains with it.

Chapter 14
ANASTASIA GOES WILD

As head of his own family, Anastasia, to the horror of Costello, proved to be even more violent than before. The case of Arnold Schuster, a salesman in Brooklyn, demonstrated this to a terrifying degree.

Arnold Schuster recognized on the New York underground a famous bank robber called Willie Sutton. Schuster called the police, who duly arrested Sutton. Schuster became the hero for the day and was interviewed by the press but, a few days later, was found dead with two bullets in the groin and one in each eye.

Anastasia had ordered the killing, stating simply: "I can't stand squealers." The hit went ahead, and the killer was also killed afterward. This insane action greatly agitated the mob, whose policy of only killing their own was generally followed.

Another strike against Anastasia was the death of his old buddy Frank Scalise, alias Don Ceech. Albert and Don had been friends from way back, but friendship is no help in the mob when money is concerned. Scalise was accused of a number of faults, ranging from selling membership in the Mafia for $50,000 a whack (and not sharing the profits) to not reimbursing his mob partners when a shipment of heroin they had paid for was captured by the police.

Whatever happened regarding Scalise's working practices, there is no doubting his end. While buying fruit at a fruit stand in the Bronx, someone cut him down with four bullets. (Aficionados will recognize an echo of this in the scene from *The Godfather* when Don Corleone is nearly killed by two thugs.)

Some have pointed the finger at Anastasia for this, stating that he ordered his old pal to be killed to show the other bosses that he would not tolerate the behavior of someone who tried to swindle his fellows. Others, with perhaps more foresight, have pointed the finger at Genovese. It is a favorite tactic of the mob to kill someone close to a gangster who is going to be hit. One of the gunmen was believed to have been Jimmy Squillante, who was known to be very close to Genovese. This theory was given credence by the fact that the brother of the deceased, Joe, started making threats about taking his revenge.

To his surprise, Anastasia seemed to be very quiet on this matter, so Joe went into hiding. He was lured out by a promise that all was well and accepted an invitation to a party thrown by Squillante.

On September 7, 1957, Joe Scalise took up the invitation and entered the abode of Mr. Squillante. The guests, led by Squillante himself, fell on him with butcher knives and cut him in pieces. The guest had the honor of having his throat cut by his host. Joe, being practically in pieces, was then put into a trash truck. (The host, obligingly, dominated the waste disposal business of the time.)

For once, natural justice took over. Squillante was charged with extortion a few years later and vanished. It was stated by most mob historians that the powers that be could not trust him to take a prison sentence. A bullet in the brain solved the problem of the trial, and the body was packed into a car, which was then crushed, and then the cube was put into a blast furnace—this solved the problem of a funeral.

With the death of his underboss, and with the rest of the bosses aghast at the behavior of the Mad Hatter, the time had come for Anastasia to go.

The fact that Anastasia tried to force Meyer Lansky to cut him in regarding a share on the fabulously profitable Cuban gambling industry did not go down very well, either. Genovese pressed for the hit to take place.

Lansky—who detested Genovese, realizing his ambition to become boss of all bosses and realizing that with Anastasia out of the way Costello would be left helpless—would probably have argued against the hit. The "little man," however, regarded Cuba as his own personal fiefdom and was, understandably, very annoyed at this thug demanding a share of the booty. Lansky voted for the hit, and as in most cases, what the little man suggested duly occurred. In this Lansky was helped by a man who matched Lansky's own cunning and ruthlessness: Carlo Gambino, the underboss to Anastasia and a man who would be regarded as the last of the genuine Godfathers.

A man described by others as "a squirrel," Gambino had borne the brunt of Anastasia's wrath on several occasions, narrowly avoiding a public beating. Being a man of unlimited ambition, he realized that Genovese was trying to take his made master out of the running. When approached by emissaries from Genovese, Gambino willingly agreed to set up his boss. With the perception of the true plotter, Gambino saw that if the hit went ahead, he would be regarded as Genovese's puppet, something that Gambino did not want in the least. With forward planning worthy of a logistical officer, Gambino not only went ahead with Genovese's idea to take out Anastasia but also started to plan the demise or incarceration of Genovese.

On October 25, 1957, Anastasia entered the barbershop of the Sheraton Hotel in New York. What happened next is of particular interest to this author, as one of the men who is believed to have taken part in the following incident was the godfather of a source this author has used on many occasions.

Anastasia's bodyguard parked the car they had arrived in and, very conveniently, went for a stroll. Anastasia settled in the barber's chair, and the barber went to work. At this point, two men, their faces covered in masks, entered the shop.

"Keep your mouth shut if you do not want your head blown off," said one of the men to the owner of the shop—an order that was followed to the letter. The pair moved to Anastasia's chair, shoving the attending barber out of the way. Anastasia still had not opened his eyes. Both men shot Anastasia, who after the first volley jumped to his feet. He lunged at his killers but only succeeded in lunging at their reflections in the mirror. Several more shots were fired, and the Lord High Executioner died in the barbershop.

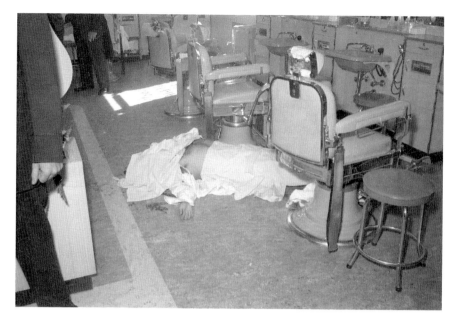

Albert Anastasia died in a barbershop. (Wags said that if he did not die in the chair, he died near to one!)

Some wags in the newspaper industry said that justice had been done; the ferocious killer who had escaped the chair decades earlier had been killed in one.

Aficionados of the mob were divided on who carried out the hit that experts such as Pittsburgh Phil regarded as very sloppy. Some suggested that it was Squillante and others that it was the homicidal Gallo brothers. Whatever the case, the Mad Hatter was no more.

Afterword

By the beginning of the 1960s, the American public was becoming aware of the existence of this thing called the Mafia. The book *The Godfather* by Mario Puzo, along with its more famous cinematic dramatization, made the Mafia a popular topic of conversation. The production by HBO of the TV series *The Sopranos* (which in England was recently voted by a poll as the most popular soap series in history) made the mob totally mainstream in American consciousness.

The leading figures of the mob in this era gradually faded from the scene. Some went quietly to their maker; the route some of the others took was rather more colorful.

Meyer "the Little Fellow" Lansky

Showing his genius for making money and survival, Lansky became, in all but name, the real Godfather of the mob after Luciano's unwanted Mediterranean holiday. Such was his skill at avoiding the limelight that he was not named in the famous Kefauver hearings that took place in America in 1950–51 that finally revealed to the American public how powerful the mob was. (The hearings, incidentally, apart from the publicity value, did not really do too much to harm the mob.) The advice from Luciano in Italy was almost invariably "listen to Meyer," with reference to the administration of the mob world.

Lansky put a large part of mob funds into the booming casinos of Cuba, which earned the mob a fortune until the coming of Castro—who, with distressingly little attention paid to the importance of the buck and a dishonest profit, shut them down. The little Jew (played as Hyman Roth by Lee Strasberg in *The Godfather Part II*) managed to accumulate a fortune in his various dealings, though he had to flee to Israel to avoid being arrested for income tax evasion. Deported on the personal orders of Golda Meir, the then Israeli prime minister, who did not think that a crime baron was altogether appropriate material for a pioneer state, Lansky went back to America, where he managed to get acquitted of an income tax charge and settled back into semiretirement, dying in 1983 and leaving a fortune estimated to be at least $380,000,000. Many of his colleagues in the syndicate would be by no means so fortunate.

BUGSY GETS HIS

That most handsome hood Bugsy Siegel was probably most relieved to hear of the death of the Kid.

Being next on the list for the New York prosecutors was not a joke for this handsome killer. Unfortunately, Siegel did not take to heart the lesson that Lansky had learned and proceeded to adopt a very high profile in California, where he had been sent to develop the gambling empire of the mob. It was either him or Lansky who first developed the idea of making Las Vegas, then a dead-end town in Nevada, into the gambling capital of the world. Investing huge amounts of his money, and the mob's, he built the magnificent Flamingo Hotel, named after his favorite mistress (he had so many that it is impossible to count them all), Virginia Hill, whose nickname it was.

A huge amount of money ($6,000,000 is the usual sum given) was sunk into it. The hotel opened to great fanfare in December 1946 and, in the opening night, lost a fortune, probably because of the crooked croupiers that Bugsy had hired—it seems they were working on the side for rival casinos. The reputation of the place could hardly have improved

Bugsy Siegel got his after being shot by an army standard carbine. (Do *not* steal from the mob.)

when a gambler thought that he had been swindled of his winnings. The croupier, who like most of the mob was a stranger to honesty, compromise and basic common sense, showed his intelligence (or lack of it) by pulling a piece from his jacket and pointing it at the gambler, along with some unrepeatable threats. The gambler proceeded to have a bowel movement that was as violent as it was unexpected.

Losing money regarding a gambling casino takes some skill, and the mob thought, probably correctly, that Bugsy was skimming, recouping both the profits and the original cash for the construction, and was placing his ill-gotten gains, with the help of Virginia, in banks in Switzerland.

As has been said before, one bad act in the mob wipes out a lifetime of good ones. Despite the fact that by 1947 the casino was making a profit, the vote was taken, with Lansky in the chair, that Bugsy had to go. On June 20, 1947, in the mansion of Virginia, who (some say not fortuitously) was away, two slugs crashed through one of the mansion's windows and into the face of the crooked thief. Siegel was killed instantly, and the prosecuting team in New York could be forgiven if they thought that justice, of a sort, had been done.

The mistress of Bugsy, the much traveled Virginia Hill, seems to have taken a liking to the Swiss Alps, which is probably why she committed suicide there in 1966.

GENOVESE: HOW NOT TO BEHAVE LIKE A GODFATHER

Genovese was becoming a threat to all, which is why—with the help of his best friend, Tony Bender—Costello, Lansky and Luciano managed to set up him and more than twenty others in a fraudulent drug deal.

Genovese, from the enforced incarceration of his prison cell, had time to think out the way he had been conned. He correctly put the blame (for the most part) on caporegime Bender. This would not have been a particularly difficult decision to come to, as Bender had already betrayed a longtime friend, Augie Pisano, who was shot in the back of a car, with Janice Drake, the wife of the comedian Alan Drake. According to a story this author has heard about, the son of the deceased gangster decided that his son, who was not yet in his teens, should learn a lesson from this rub out. He took his son to where his grandfather's corpse was and said to him: "Learn a lesson from this, son, this is what happens when your guard drops!"

Bender, who had been very close to Genovese—who himself had been the best man at Bender's wedding—suffered the fate of the Sicilian-inspired Lupara Bianca (the white shotgun), disappearing without a trace in 1962. Rumors differ as to whether this devious rogue is not part of the foundations for a skyscraper or a motorway somewhere.

Genovese stayed in prison long enough to ruminate on the folly of taking on too many enemies and died in prison in 1970, "the Boss of Bosses" who never was.

FRANK COSTELLO: THE PRIME MINISTER OF THE MOB

The urbane Costello, more than any other man in the mob, was probably responsible for the Kid taking his flying lesson. Doc Stacher, a leading mobster, stated with reference to the Kid, apropos Costello:

> *He got to work and found out which room Reles was in at the Half Moon Hotel* [the Coney Island hotel where Reles was, supposedly, held under round-the-clock supervision]. *This was not so hard, as the cops had a guard on it; but then Frank really showed his muscle. He knew so many top-ranking cops, that he got the names of the detectives who were guarding Reles. We never asked exactly how he did it, but one evening he came in with a smile and said, "It's cost us a hundred grand, but Kid Reles is about to join his maker!"*

Like Lansky, Costello was a good deal more intelligent than some of the thugs who surrounded him. This was shown in his friendship with FBI chief J. Edgar Hoover, who was given tips by "Uncle Frank" at the racetracks, which Hoover loved to visit. The quid pro quo for this strange arrangement was that Hoover would not interfere with the gambling activities of the mob. He didn't.

Apart from a couple of relatively unimportant incarcerations for income tax evasion, Costello began to feel threatened by Genovese—a very bad showing on the Kefauver hearings did not help here—which was confirmed when he was nearly taken out by Don Vito in 1957. With the help of Lansky and Luciano, Costello put one over on Genovese, who was sent to prison on a framed-up drug charge in 1959. Costello was briefly in the same prison in Atlanta to which he had sent Don Vito, and the two were said to have had a sentimental reconciliation. (Believe that and you will believe anything.) In his last years, Uncle Frank appears to have led the life of a country squire, dying in comparative obscurity in 1973. None of his old buddies was invited to the funeral, which was enlivened by a cousin of his asking his widow what she would be doing with Frank's clothes. Mrs. Costello did not answer this question, which was something, in the words of mob historian Carl Sifakis, that Costello would have appreciated.

Charles "Lucky" Luciano

Luciano is the epitome of the old truth that there is no honor among thieves—or at least there are some very strange examples of it.

After being incarcerated for fifty years for prostitution charges, Luciano was released in rather strange circumstances. In 1942, the great French liner *Normandie* was burned and made useless in the New York docks. The story was rapidly passed around—which was probably completely erroneous—that the fire was the work of saboteurs. The navy was put in contact with Luciano, who was reported to have told them that if they helped let him out of prison, he would stop the trouble on the docks. Luciano was released and exiled to Italy in 1946, the sabotage on the docks apparently having come to an end.

It appears that the burning down of the *Normandie* was the work of men in the employ of Albert Anastasia, who ordered the act to blackmail the government into letting Luciano out of prison. (Loyalty to some of his friends was one of the very few virtues Anastasia possessed.) Luciano was released, therefore, as a result of a monumental conning of the American republic. Another strange story, which has somehow received some credence, was that Luciano drew maps of the island of Sicily to help the Allies invade the place in 1943. How a man who had not been to Sicily since he left as a child, and was without any cartographical or surveying experience, could draw maps of this area is beyond this writer's imagination.

Luciano's stay in Italy was not uncomfortable, since it seems that $25,000 was delivered to him each month, sometimes by the much traveled Ms. Hill.

His influence began to wane toward the end of the 1950s, and in an attempt to earn some more cash he began to talk to journalists about his past exploits. This did not please the leading members of the mob at this time (Lansky), and when Luciano died of a heart attack in Naples airport in 1962, some said that it was only a matter of time before Lansky's assassins got to him, anyway.

ABNER "LONGY" ZWILLMAN

One of the leading members of the syndicate, Zwillman ruled with such effectiveness in New Jersey that he was called the Al Capone of that state.

Possessed of the usual cunning associated with a mob boss, it was he who helped stitch up the deal that sent Buchalter on his wild goose chase into the unappealing arms of J. Edgar Hoover and, by natural progression, to his shocking ending in Sing Sing.

Unlike Lansky and Costello, time did not treat Longy well. He picked the wrong side in the Anastasia/Genovese standoff and began to be troubled by the Internal Revenue Service. A mob leader, like any other leader, is never so weak as when his colleagues think he is, which is why the other families began to stake a claim to the businesses in New Jersey.

Genovese also thought that Longy had helped send him away on the drug scam. Zwillman replied to these threats in an odd way: he committed suicide.

Not only was this an unusual way to solve his problems, but the many cynics were also rather bewildered as to the technique of his termination. Longy had managed to commit suicide by strangling himself with a plastic rope. Scratches were also found on his hands, which seemed to show that they had been tied up with wire. Some say that the means of his death were quite simple: if Longy had been tried and found guilty, he might have started singing to get a reduced sentence, à la Reles. So, some experts were sent to Longy's house, told him that his time had come, gave him a bottle of very expensive brandy to drink and then suspended the reluctant hood from a water pipe. *Sic transit gloria mundi.*

TONY BENDER

With his former boss in prison, Bender, with his usual chameleon-like ability to change sides, thought that he was now secure under the aegis of Gambino. Unfortunately, Genovese, who now had considerable time on his hands, slowly worked out the manner in which he had been set up. By some byzantine calculations, he realized that Bender had helped set him up. It was also discovered that Bender was feathering his own nest at his old boss's expense. The author must once again stress that this would be regarded as being unforgivable, the mob being concerned with making money above all.

Bender was dealt with in 1962. Going out of his house one day, he was warned to wrap up tightly, as it was cold outside. "Don't worry," said Bender. "I'm wearing thermal underwear." He walked out of the house and was never seen again. The established knowledge was that he was killed and buried under the foundations of a New York skyscraper; my source says that he is actually at the bottom of a lake in New Jersey.

JOE GALLO

The purported hit man who helped take out Anastasia, Joe Gallo served numerous sentences in prison, where he educated himself and read the works of Balzac, Camus and Sartre (he deserves a medal for the last one). After leaving the pen, he sought out the company of writers and scriptwriters, advised on how to make a film about the mob and seemed on his way to becoming a celebrity. His ending, though, was one of the most famous in gangland history. One of the author's sources was Gallo's godson, and he passed on some of the following facts.

On April 7, 1972, Gallo, his bodyguard Pete "the Greek" Diapoulas and four friends went to Umberto's Clamhouse in the Little Italy area of New York. There appeared to be a code of the mob that rub outs never occurred in this particular area; as usual, whenever the circumstances dictated, this was ignored. Gallo appeared to have a premonition of this, since before a visit to the men's room he told his bodyguard that he "had a funny feeling."

This was proven to be correct, since a man walked into the restaurant (according to my source, it was someone called Joey Pinto) and started blasting at Joe. Joe ran out of the restaurant, the man pursued him, still firing, and crazy Joe Gallo, like the mobsters in so many films, died in the street.

Sources Consulted

Cohen, Rich. *Tough Jews: Fathers, Sons, and Gangster Dreams*. New York: Vintage Publishing, 1999.

Rockaway, Robert A. *But He Was Good to His Mother: The Lives and Crimes of Jewish Gangsters*. Jerusalem, Israel: Gefen Publishing, 2000.

Sifakis, Carl. *The Mafia Encyclopedia*. New York: Checkmark Books, 2005.

Turkus, Burton. *Murder Inc.: The Story of the Syndicate*. Jackson, TN: Da Capo Press, 2003.